English Grammar

Second Edition

English Grammar

Open Road

Second Edition

Lynne Gaetz

PEARSON
Longman

DISTRIBUTED IN CANADA BY ERPI
5757, RUE CYPIHOT, SAINT-LAURENT (QUÉBEC) H4S 1R3
TELEPHONE: **(514) 334-2690** ext. 232   FAX: **(514) 334-0448**
infoesl@erpi.com   **w w w . l o n g m a n e s l . c a**

ACKNOWLEDGEMENTS

I would like to express sincere thanks to:

- Lucie Turcotte for her patience and insights while editing this book
- Sharnee Chait and Jeremy Lanaway for their invaluable editing
- Dominique Gagnon and the team at Dessine-moi un mouton
- My students and colleagues at College Lionel-Groulx

Finally, I extend special thanks to my husband and children.

Managing Editor
Sharnee Chait

Editor
Lucie Turcotte

Copy Editor
Jeremy Lanaway

Proofreader
My-Trang Nguyen

Art Director
Hélène Cousineau

Cover, book design and page layout
Dessine-moi un mouton

CREDITS

p. 7 Ladies' Whalebone Corset © Underwood Photo Archives / SuperStock. p. 14 Wallis Simpson and King Edward VIII © Cecil Beaton / Camera Press / PONOPRESSE. p. 18 King Henry VIII of England © Stock Montage / SuperStock. p. 28 King Kong (1933) © SuperStock, Inc. p. 35 Sean Connery as James Bond (1964) © SuperStock, Inc. p. 38 Charlie Chaplin in *The Gold Rush* (1925) © Culver Pictures, Inc. / SuperStock. p. 42 Cleopatra VII (69-30 B.C.), Queen of Egypt © Stock Montage / SuperStock. p. 60 Businessman © SuperStock, Inc. p. 76 Car salesman © Francisco Cruz / SuperStock. p. 82 Self-portrait (1907) by Pablo Picasso (1981-1973; Spanish). Oil on canvas; Narodni Gallery, Prague. © Picasso Estate / SODRAC (2007). Photograph from SuperStock. p. 83 "The Two Saltimbanques" (Harlequin and His Companion) (1901) by Pablo Picasso (1881-1973; Spanish). Oil on canvas, Pushkin Museum, Moscow. © Picasso Estate / SODRAC (2007). Photograph from SuperStock. p. 97 Photograph © iStockphoto. p. 109 Migrant Mother by Dorothea Lange © 2005 Gettyimages. p. 112 Untitled painting (1912) by Suzanne Valadon (1867-1938; French) © Estate of Suzanne Valadon / SODRAC (2007). Photograph from SuperStock. p. 125 China's Unknown Rebel © AP Images / Ben Devries.

Registration of copyright: Bibliothèque et Archives nationales du Québec 2007
Registration of copyright: Library and Archives Canada 2007

ISBN 978-2-7613-1904-1

56789 HLN 13 12 11
10811 ABCD OF-10

Table of Contents
Open Road English Grammar, Second Edition

Subject-Verb Agreement and Tense Consistency

Subject-Verb Agreement

One of the most common errors made by second-language learners involves subject-verb agreement. To perfect your English, you should master the skill of making your subjects and verbs agree.

There are two forms of present tense verbs: the base form and the third-person singular form. Use the base form when the subject is *I, you, we,* or *they.*

> <u>Politicians</u> **want** people to believe them. I know that <u>you</u> **have** your doubts about all political figures because <u>we</u> **discuss** politics every week.

Add *-s* or *-es* to verbs that follow *he, she,* or *it.* In other words, if the subject is one person, place, or thing, but not *you* or *I,* the verb must take the *-s* or *-es* ending.

> One person: <u>Mr. Roy</u> **believes** in ghosts.
>
> One place: The <u>museum</u> **displays** many exhibits.
>
> One thing: The <u>box</u> **contains** photos.

Special Subjects

Gerunds

Sometimes a gerund (*-ing* form of the verb) is the singular subject of a sentence.

> <u>Snowboarding</u> requires good reflexes.

Indefinite Pronouns

Indefinite pronouns beginning with *every, some, any,* and *no* are considered singular. To help you remember this rule, notice that the last part of each word is a singular subject.

Singular indefinite pronouns:

everybody	everyone	everything	everywhere
somebody	someone	something	somewhere
nobody	no one	nothing	nowhere

> <u>Everyone</u> **has** fears, but <u>nobody</u> **likes** to admit it.

If you put one or more singular nouns (joined by *and*) after *each* and *every,* the verb remains singular.

> <u>Every</u> person in the room **needs** help. <u>Each</u> man and woman **talks** about it.

Spelling Rules

Add -*es* to verbs ending in *s*, *sh*, *ss*, *ch*, *o*, or *x*.

teach 〉 teach**es**   do 〉 do**es**

Change *y* to *ies* when verbs end in consonant + *y*.

carry 〉 carr**ies**   study 〉 stud**ies**

Keep the *y* and add -*s* when the verb ends in vowel + *y*.

say 〉 say**s**   destroy 〉 destroy**s**

EXERCISE 1 〉 Underline and correct the errors involving subject-verb agreement. There are fifteen verbs to conjugate in total.

has
Example: Margo <u>have</u> strange opinions about urban legends.

1 • Urban legends <u>is</u> *are* stories about frightening events. Everyone share similar fears. Usually, somebody say that the story happened to a friend of a friend. Believing such stories require a certain level of gullibility.

2 • Every man and woman know an urban legend. Each urban legend <u>serve</u> *serves* a purpose. It is about ordinary people in frightening situations, and each legend <u>warn</u> *warns* us about a possible danger. Sometimes a story <u>have</u> *has* a moral. Additionally, when someone tell a story about a scary or traumatic event, the story <u>release</u> *releases* collective anxiety.

3 • Many urban legends <u>is</u> *are* very old. For example, the "earwig" legend is over one thousand years old. Nobody <u>know</u> *knows* where the story began. In the story, an earwig look for a dark place to hide. It crawl into a person's ear to lay eggs. The eggs hatch, and tiny earwigs eat the person's brain. Perhaps people repeat this story because they <u>is</u> *are* afraid of insects.

Past Tense Agreement

In the past tense, almost all verbs have one past form, so you don't have to modify them when the subject changes. The only past tense verb that requires subject-verb agreement is the verb *be*, which has two past forms: *was* and *were*.

I / He / She / It **was** in the living room.

You / We / They **were** in the kitchen.

There + Be

When sentences begin with *There*, the real subject follows the verb *be*.

There **is / was** + one thing.   There **was** <u>a fire</u> on Elm Street.

There **are / were** + two or more things   There **were** <u>many firefighters</u> at the site.

EXERCISE 2 ❯ Underline the appropriate verbs in parentheses.

Example: Everybody (<u>has</u> / have) an opinion on the role of religion in schools.

1• In 1859, Charles Darwin wrote *The Origin of the Species*. In Victorian England, Darwin's ideas (was / <u>were</u>) regarded as a threat to Christianity. Sixty-six years later, the Theory of Evolution (<u>was</u> / were) still controversial. In 1925, in many southern states, teachers (was / <u>were</u>) not permitted to teach evolution. In Tennessee, for example, some (was / <u>were</u>) brave enough to break the law and teach Darwin's theories, but they did so in contravention of the "Butler Act." According to the Butler Act, if anybody (teach / <u>teaches</u>) a theory that denies the story of divine creation, it is unlawful.

2• In 1925, John Scopes (<u>was</u> / were) a twenty-four-year-old biology teacher who taught evolution. There (was / <u>were</u>) many people who wanted the Butler Act to be debated in court, so Scopes agreed to go to trial. His trial, which became known as the "Monkey Trial," (<u>was</u> / were) in newspapers around the world. Gossiping about the case (<u>was</u> / were) common in newsrooms. The Scopes Trial lasted for fifteen days, and nobody (<u>was</u> / were) prepared for defence lawyer Clarence Darrow's decision. He asked the jury to find his client guilty because he wanted to take the case to Tennessee's Supreme Court. The jury members (was / <u>were</u>) surprised, but they agreed to make a guilty verdict. Scopes and his lawyer (was / <u>were</u>) happy with the outcome because there (<u>was</u> / were) a lively discussion about evolution in the media.

More Than One Subject

There are special agreement rules when a sentence contains more than one subject.

And, Or, and *Nor*

When two or more subjects are joined by *and*, use the plural form of the verb. However, when subjects are joined by *or* or *nor*, the verb agrees with the subject closest to it.

plural

Neither Anna nor her <u>children</u> **watch** television.

singular

Either the children or <u>Clara</u> **is** allergic to dust.

EXERCISE 3 ❯ Underline and correct eight errors involving subject-verb agreement in the following paragraphs.

are
Example: There <u>is</u> some interesting legends about the Bermuda Triangle.

1 • In 1872, a ship called the *Mary Celeste* left New York Harbour. Captain Benjamin Briggs, as well as his family and eight crew members, were on the ship. Later, the

was
ship was found floating in the sea. It was in good condition, but nobody <u>were</u> on it.

were
Neither the Captain nor the crew members <u>was</u> anywhere near the ship.

are
2 • Today, there <u>is</u> many theories about the *Mary Celeste*. Some *suggests* suggest that perhaps

was
strong winds or a giant rainstorm <u>were</u> responsible for the missing crew members.

Perhaps either one or several crew members was violent and murderous. Maybe

was   *Does*
everybody <u>were</u> captured by aliens. <u>Do</u> anyone know what really happened?

Collective Nouns

Collective nouns refer to a group of people or things. Here are some common collective nouns.

army	class	crowd	group	public
association	club	family	jury	organization
audience	committee	gang	mob	society
band	company	government	population	team

Generally, each group acts as a unit, so you must use the singular form of the verb.

The <u>jury</u> **is** ready to read the verdict.

If the members of the group act individually, use the plural form of the verb.
It is a good idea to reword the sentence using a phrase such as *members of*.

(acceptable) The <u>jury</u> **are** not able to come to an agreement.

(better)   The <u>members of the jury</u> **are** not able to come to an agreement.

 Tip

Police Is Considered Plural
The word *police* is thought of as a plural noun because the word *officers* is implied but not stated.

The police **have** a protester in custody.

EXERCISE 4 ❯ Underline the appropriate verbs in parentheses.

Example: In many communities around the world, people (<u>believe</u> / believes) in ghosts.

1 • In *The Power of Myth*, Joseph Campbell (state / <u>states</u>), "A fairytale is the child's myth. There (is / <u>are</u>) proper myths for proper times of life. As you (<u>grow</u> / grows) older, you (<u>need</u> / needs) a sturdier mythology." Every society (invent / <u>invents</u>) stories to try to understand basic truths.

2 • In the Chinese lunar tradition, the seventh month (<u>is</u> / are) "ghost month." During ghost month, a gate (separate / <u>separates</u>) the spirit world from the normal world. It (open / <u>opens</u>), and the spirits (enter / <u>enters</u>) the human world. Buddhist priests (<u>pray</u> / prays) to subdue the spirits. A band (play / <u>plays</u>) music to welcome the spirits, and the crowd (<u>listen</u> / listens) with reverence. In Taiwan, a typical family (welcome / <u>welcomes</u>) the ghosts during ghost month. Feeding the ghosts (<u>is</u> / are) common. Lanterns (<u>show</u> / shows) the ghosts the way to the banquet tables.

3 • Each nation (have / <u>has</u>) its own version of ghost stories. As long as everyone (have / <u>has</u>) questions about death and the afterlife, religious scholars will continue to examine the spirit world.

Interrupting Words and Phrases

Words that come between the subject and the verb can cause confusion. In such cases, look for the subject and then make sure that the verb agrees with it.

Some <u>books</u> that I read in my first college course **are** about ghosts.

Prepositional Phrases

A **prepositional phrase** is made up of a preposition and its object (a noun or a pronoun). The object of the prepositional phrase is <u>not</u> the subject of the sentence. In the following sentences, the subject and verb are interrupted by a prepositional phrase.

The <u>man</u> with the tattoos **has** red hair.

Be particularly careful with phrases containing *of the*. In the next examples, the subject appears before *of the*.

<u>One</u> of the most annoying neighbours in our district **knows** everybody's secrets.

A <u>photo</u> of the cars **appears** in the magazine.

<u>Each</u> of the photos **is** in colour.

Exception: Expressions of Quantity

Expressions of quantity don't follow the preceding *of the* rule. When the subject is an expression of quantity—*the majority of, one-third of, a part of, ten percent of, the rest of*—the verb agrees with the noun that follows *of the*.

The majority of the <u>shareholders</u> **want** another president.

The majority of the <u>audience</u> **likes** the show.

About 20 percent of the <u>viewers</u> **watch** the program each week.

EXERCISE 5 Underline and correct twelve errors involving subject-verb agreement. If you aren't sure about a particular verb, try to identify the subject of the sentence.

                                 encounter
    Example: About 30 percent of travellers <u>encounters</u> problems.

1. The majority of people <u>likes</u> to travel. In 2006, Natalia Macdonald went to Africa to work in a camp for AIDS orphans. She left the capital of Ghana and rode on a bus to the town of Manya Krobo. She noticed that some of the villages <u>was</u> large *were* and had schools, stores, and houses, but the majority *were* was small and consisted of around twenty little mud huts. The roads <u>were</u> a dark orange colour, and one of the most incredible sights <u>were</u> the numerous huge anthills that were formed from the orange dirt. Each anthill <u>were</u> about three-feet high! Her photograph of the anthills <u>was</u> very impressive.

2. According to statistics, about 12 percent of travellers <u>has</u> bad experiences during their vacations. Good planning helps a traveller <u>avoids</u> many problems. For instance, a map that indicates the main hotels are useful.

3. When you travel, if someone makes you <u>feels</u> nervous, listen to your instincts. You don't have to take unnecessary chances. There <u>is</u> a lot of ways to travel safely! Certainly the majority of strangers <u>is</u> not planning to rob you. Nevertheless, if someone seem suspicious, be careful.

Tense Consistency

Avoiding Tense Shifts

When you write, don't shift tenses unless the time frame really changes. In the example below, the first sentence is a generalization, while the next three sentences are part of a past tense story.

> I **believe** in bad luck. Last Saturday, I **walked** under a ladder. Suddenly, bad things **began** to happen. First, I **slipped** while I **was carrying** a tray at work. Then I **cut** my finger.

Tip

Would and *Could*

When you tell a story about a past event, use *would* instead of *will* and *could* instead of *can*.

     would   could not

In 1950, women ~~will~~ wear cashmere sweaters. Men ~~cannot~~ have long hair during those years. If a man grew a ponytail, others ridiculed him.

EXERCISE 6 ❯ Underline and correct ten errors involving tense shifts.

         didn't

Example: In 1938, he dieted, but he <u>doesn't</u> lose much weight.

1• In the nineteenth century, extremely small waists were popular, so some women will have their lower ribs removed. Then they will wear tight corsets. Many women cannot breathe properly with their tight corsets, and they often lost consciousness.

2• Another unhealthy beauty regime involved arsenic. In the seventeenth century, many wealthy Europeans <u>want</u> *wanted* to look pale and sickly. A suntan was considered vulgar because people of the lower classes worked outdoors and have tans. Sometimes wealthy people took small amounts of arsenic to make their skin look pale.

3• In the past, men also paid attention to appearances. When King Louis XIV began to lose his hair, he wore elaborate wigs. Soon fashionable men of France thought that they will look better with a wig.

4• Over two hundred years ago, barbers did dental work in addition to hair cutting. They used nitric acid to whiten people's teeth. The acid worked well, although it can also remove the enamel from teeth. Many people's teeth decayed after the whitening treatments.

5• In the 1950s, cosmetic surgery became popular. Marilyn Monroe, for example, has a nose job at the beginning of her career so that her face will look more beautiful. Today, many people still chose to go under the surgeon's knife.

Writing About Fiction

When writing about a fictional short story or novel, use the present tense to describe the characters and their situations.

> In F. Scott Fitzgerald's story, Bernice **feels** shy and awkward around boys.
> She **receives** some advice from her cousin, Marjorie.

When writing about historical events, use the past tense.

> In the 1920s, young people **socialized** at dinner parties and in dance clubs.

Ensure that your tenses are consistent and do not shift when you write about fiction.

EXERCISE 7 ❯ Underline and correct ten errors involving tense shifts.

1 • In the nineteenth century, men and women lived in different spheres. They could meet in public places, but young men and women can't go on dates unless a chaperone was present. Women are considered morally superior to men at that time, but when a man seduced a woman, she will receive the blame. By the 1920s, non-chaperoned dating became common and acceptable, and young people openly flirted with the opposite sex.

2 • In 1920s jazz clubs, youths ~~meet~~ *met* one another and dance. A girl was popular if many boys "cut in" on her ~~dances.~~ *dance.* In F. Scott Fitzgerald's short story, "Bernice Bobs Her Hair," Bernice is initially unpopular. Boys didn't want to dance with her. Then she receives some advice from her cousin, Marjorie. Her cousin wanted Bernice to be more popular, so she gave her a lot of advice. Bernice learns to entertain her dance partners with sparkling conversation, and they soon felt comfortable around her. Bernice becomes popular, but when she decided to cut her hair, her friends desert her.

❯ Take Another Look

Answer the following questions. If you don't know an answer, go back and review the appropriate section.

1 • When should you add *-s* or *-es* to verbs? *simple present after he/she/it*

2 • Some indefinite pronouns are singular and require the singular form of the verb. List six singular indefinite pronouns.

everybody   everyone   everywhere
something   someone   somewhere

3 • Some nouns are collective and require the singular form of the verb. Circle five collective nouns.

(army)   (committee)   (family)   people
brothers   (crowd)   judge   (population)

4 • When do you use *was* and *were*?

a) Use *was* _singular_

b) Use *were* _plural_

5 • Correct the errors involving subject-verb agreement in the following sentences.

a) There ~~is~~ many different religions. *are*

b) Either the Edwards sisters or Simon ~~are~~ in the room. *is*

c) One of our cousins ~~live~~ in Thailand. *lives*

d) The majority of the people ~~has~~ a television. *have*

Final Review

Part A

Underline the appropriate verbs in parentheses.

Example: In many myths and legends, people (is / **are**) either good or evil.

1 • Some authors realize that both good and evil (exists / **exist**) in all of us. One of the best books about this topic (**was** / were) popular in 1886. Robert Louis Stevenson illustrated this duality of good and evil in his novel *The Strange Case of Dr. Jekyll and Mr. Hyde*. When the book was first published, there (was / **were**) some critics who disliked it. Today, just about every man and woman (**know** / knows) the story.

2 • The hero of the story is Dr. Jekyll. He is a scientist who everybody (respect / **respects**). Learning about personality traits (**is** / are) his passion. Dr. Jekyll, away from the prying eyes of others, (drink / **drinks**) a powerful potion. He (don't / **doesn't**) know what will happen. His personality, usually very sweet and friendly, (change / **changes**) completely, and the mild doctor (become / **becomes**) the evil Mr. Hyde. Neither his cook nor his butler (**understand** / understands) what is going on.

3 • One night, a murder occurs and the police (is / **are**) near the crime scene. One of the officers (speak / **speaks**) to possible witnesses, but nobody really (know / **knows**) who the murderer is. A painting of two possible suspects (hang / **hangs**) on a nearby wall. Then one of the officers (find / **finds**) a letter on the body. The letter is for a lawyer called Utterson.

4 • Two police officers (speak / speaks) with the lawyer who then (lead / leads) them to the home of Dr. Jekyll. When they enter the house, neither the lawyer nor the officers (expect / expects) to find the murderer. What they find (is / are) the pale, thin Dr. Jekyll in his laboratory. Everybody quickly (realize / realizes) that the doctor is very ill. What nobody (know / knows), however, is that Dr. Jekyll is also the murderous Mr. Hyde.

5 • In the novel, both characters (reside / resides) within the same man. Robert Louis Stevenson shows us a shocking truth—that good as well as evil (exist / exists) within us. The majority of readers (enjoy / enjoys) the novel.

Part B
Underline and correct five errors involving tense shifts in the following paragraph.

6 • In the summer of 1816, the poet Lord Byron was at his Swiss villa entertaining guests. His visitors <u>include</u> *(included)* the poet Percy Shelley and his nineteen-year-old wife Mary. One stormy night, they <u>cannot</u> *(could not)* go outside because the weather was so miserable. Instead, the group decided that they will have a contest. The guest who could write the best ghost story <u>will win</u> *(wins)*. Mary Shelley wrote about a professor who <u>created</u> *(creates)* a strange creature out of body parts. When she was just twenty-one, she published her novel *Frankenstein*. Later, the novel <u>will become</u> *(became)* wildly successful.

Present, Past, and Future Tenses

The Present Tenses

Compare the simple present and the present progressive tenses.

The baby **sleeps** for ten hours every night. (simple present)

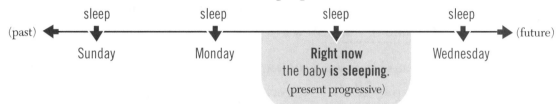

the baby **is sleeping**.
(present progressive)

Present Tense Forms

	SIMPLE PRESENT (GENERAL)	PRESENT PROGRESSIVE (NOW)
Form	I, You, We, They } like He, She, It } like**s**	I } am He, She, It } is You, We, They } are + <u>verb</u> -ing
Usage	Indicates general truths, facts, and habitual actions. 　Mr. Wade **owns** a company. (fact) 　I **play** tennis once a month. (habit) **Key words:** always, often, usually, sometimes, seldom, rarely, never, every day …	Indicates that an action is happening now, or for a present, temporary period of time. 　Right now we **are eating** lunch. (now) 　This week Ann **is visiting** us. (temporary period of time) **Key words:** now, at this moment, currently, today, these days, this week, this month, this morning … **Note:** Always check the context. For example, look at the following sentence: 　When I was in high school, I always ate junk food, but now I eat well. (*Now* refers to a general present time, not to this specific moment.)
Question	Put *do* or *does* before the subject. Use the base form of the verb. 　Why **does** she always complain? 　What **do** you want? Exception: *be* 　Why **is** Julie late? 　Where **are** the tennis balls?	Put *be* before the subject. 　**Am** I bothering you? 　**Is** she sleeping now? 　**Are** they staying with us?
Negative	Add *do* or *does* with *not*. 　Julie **does not** complain. (doesn't) 　They **do not** own a company. (don't) Exception: *be* 　They are **not** late. (aren't)	Add *not*. 　He is **not** sleeping right now. (isn't) 　They are **not** working these days. (aren't)

The Simple Present and the Present Progressive

EXERCISE 1 ❭ Underline the correct verb forms in parentheses below. Then identify the usage of the verbs. Write *G* if the verb refers to a general fact or habit. Write *N* if it refers to an action that is happening now or for a temporary period of time.

Example: What (<u>is he reading</u> / does he read) _N_ right now?

1• Every week, Alan (is having / have / <u>has</u>) _G_ a history class. His professor is quite well known, and she often (is giving / give / <u>gives</u>) _G_ interviews to the local media. Today, the professor (<u>is talking</u> / talk / talks) _N_ to her students about past wars. According to the professor, people (are needing / <u>need</u> / needs) _G_ to remember the mistakes that previous governments made. During class, the students often (are watching / <u>watch</u> / watches) _G_ documentary films. For example, right now they (<u>are viewing</u> / view / viewing) _N_ a film about the trenches of World War I.

2• In Alan's class, some students (<u>are currently developing</u> / currently develop) _N_ a video project about the average student's knowledge of history. The professor (meet / is meeting / <u>meets</u>) _G_ with the students on a regular basis.

> **Tip**
>
> **Question Form**
> When the main verb is a form of *be*, don't add *do* to the question form.
>
> When you add *does* to third-person singular questions, remove the final *s* from the verb.
>
>   Are you
> **Example:** ~~Do you are~~ angry?
>
>   write
> **Example:** Why does Scott ~~writes~~ novels?

EXERCISE 2 ❭ Write the contracted negative form of the verbs in the spaces provided. Then write information questions. The answers to the questions are in bold.

Example: Jonas has **three children**. _doesn't have_

Question: _How many children does Jonas have?_

1• The oldest human resides **in Florida**. _doesn't reside_

Question: _Where resides the oldest human?_

2• He is **122 years** old. _isn't_

Question: _How old is he?_

3• He remembers **World War I**. _doesn't remember_

Question: _What does he remember?_

4• He is playing **golf** today. _isn't_

Question: _What is he playing today?_

5• Jonas has **forty** great-grandchildren. _hasn't_

Question: _How many gr.grand. does Jonas has?_

          UNIT 2 ·· Present, Past, and Future Tenses

The Past Tenses

Compare the simple past and the past progressive tenses.

Yesterday, Tamayo <u>was cleaning</u> his studio when the fire started.

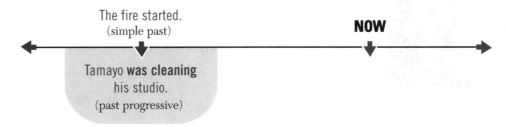

The fire started.
(simple past)

NOW

Tamayo **was cleaning**
his studio.
(past progressive)

Past Tense Forms

	SIMPLE PAST		PAST PROGRESSIVE
Form	Regular (add *-ed*) *watch* ❯ *watched*	Irregular *know* ❯ *knew*	I, He, She, It } was + <u>verb</u> *-ing* You, We, They } were
Usage	Indicates that an action was completed at a definite time in the past. Last week, I **bought** a car. **Key words:** yesterday morning, last week, when I was a child, many years ago, once upon a time ...		Indicates that an action was 1. in progress at a specific past time Yesterday at I p.m., we **were eating** lunch. 2. in progress when another activity interrupted it. While we **were eating** lunch, the phone rang. **Key words:** as, while, during
Question	Put *did* before the subject. Use the base form of the verb. Why **did** she miss the bus? Exception: *be* Why **was** Julie late? Why **were** the students absent?		Put *be* before the subject. **Was** she sleeping when the phone rang? **Were** they bothering her at 6 a.m.?
Negative	Add *did* with *not*. They **did not** finish the job. (didn't) Exception: *be* She was **not** late. (wasn't) The students were **not** absent. (weren't)		Add *not*. She was **not** sleeping when the phone rang. (wasn't) They were **not** bothering her at 6 a.m. (weren't)

EXERCISE 3 ❯ Write the verbs in parentheses in the simple past or past progressive tense.

Example: In 1936, the British people (expect) *expected* Edward VIII to become the next king.

1• In the 1920s, Edward VIII (be) <u>was</u> an eligible bachelor. One day, while he (drink) <u>was drinking</u> wine at a party, he (meet) <u>met</u> a married American woman named Wallis Simpson. Mrs. Simpson and Edward (become) <u>became</u> lovers.

>>> Wallis Simpson and King Edward VIII

2. On January 30, 1936, Edward's father, King George V, (die) ___died___ and Edward (become) ___became___ the king. Later, on a rainy morning while Edward (read) ___was reading___ a newspaper, Wallis called. She (tell) ___told___ Edward that her divorce was complete. Edward (propose) ___proposed___ to Wallis. Unfortunately, in 1936, British kings (have, not) ___didn't have___ the right to marry divorced women.

3. Edward (decide) ___decided___ that Wallis (be) ___was___ ___ more important to him than his role as king. After just 325 days as king, Edward abdicated the throne. One afternoon, while the British people (drink) ___were drinking___ afternoon tea, they (hear) ___heard___ the shocking news. Edward's brother, George VI, was the new king.

4. In 1937, Edward and Wallis (get) ___got___ married in France. The day after their wedding, while Wallis (relax) ___was relaxing___, Edward (interrupt) ___interrupted___ her. "What shall we do now?" he asked. The couple (spend) ___spent___ the next years doing very little indeed.

EXERCISE 4 > Write the contracted negative form of each verb. Then write information questions. The answers to the questions are in bold.

Example: Charlie Chaplin met **his father**. ___didn't meet___
Question: ___Who did Charlie Chaplin meet?___

1. Charlie Chaplin was from **Wales**. ___wasn't___
Question: ___Where was he from?___

2. His mother was living **in London** when Charlie was born. ___wasn't___
Question: ___Where was living his mother when C. was born?___

3. Chaplin went to America **to find work**. ___didn't go___
Question: ___Why does Chaplin went to America___

4. He did comedy routines with **his brother**. ___didn't___
Question: ___With who did he does comedy routines?___

5. Mack Sennet hired Charlie **in 1912**. ___didn't hire___
Question: ___When does Mack Sennet hired Charlie?___

UNIT 2 ·· Present, Past, and Future Tenses   © Pearson Longman – Reproduction prohibited

Spelling of *-ing* and *-ed* Verb Forms

BASE FORM	*-ING*	*-ED*	SPELLING RULES
smoke	smok**ing**	smoke**d**	*-ING*: Drop the *e* and add *-ing*. *-ED*: When verbs end in *e*, simply add *-d*.
ONE-SYLLABLE VERBS			
stop	stop**ping**	stop**ped**	When one-syllable verbs end in a consonant-vowel-consonant combination, double the last letter and add *-ing* or *-ed*.
TWO-SYLLABLE VERBS			
visit offer	visit**ing** offer**ing**	visit**ed** offer**ed**	When the final syllable is <u>not</u> stressed in verbs ending in a consonant-vowel-consonant combination, add *-ing* or *-ed*.
refer omit	refer**ring** omit**ting**	refer**red** omit**ted**	When the final syllable is stressed in verbs ending in a consonant-vowel-consonant combination, double the last letter and add *-ing* or *-ed*.
VERBS ENDING IN *Y* OR *IE*			
enjoy	enjoy**ing**	enjoy**ed**	When verbs end in vowel + *y*, just add *-ing* or *-ed*.
worry carry	worry**ing** carry**ing**	worr**ied** carr**ied**	When verbs end in consonant + *y*, just add *-ing*. However, in the past tense, change *y* to *i* and add *-ed*.
tie	**ty**ing	tie**d**	When verbs end in *ie*, change *ie* to *y* and add *-ing*. In the past tense, just add *-d*.

Exceptions: Never double the last letter of verbs ending in *w* or *x*. (*snowing, fixing*)
Quit (two vowels) becomes *qui**tt**ing*.

Tip

Use Your Dictionary
If you are not sure which syllable is stressed in a multi-syllable word, use your dictionary. Most dictionaries have stress marks indicating which sound is strongest. The stress mark often appears in the word's phonetic pronunciation.

   'of•fer   re•'fer

Thus, when you write the progressive or past forms of *offer* or *refer*, they would be written as follows:

   offering / offered   referring / referred

EXERCISE 5 For each of the following verbs, write:
- the present participle (*-ing* form);
- the simple past form. Note that some of the verbs have irregular simple past forms.

   Example: carry   *carrying*   *carried* .

   1 • try   *trying*   *tied*

2 • stay	staying	stayed
3 • study	studying	studied
4 • marry	marrying	married
5 • write	writing	wrote
6 • plan	planning	planned
7 • shop	shopping	shopped
8 • smile	smiling	smiled
9 • fall	falling	fell
10 • feel	feeling	felt
11 • happen	happening	happened
12 • begin	beginning	began
13 • question	questioning	questioned
14 • deliver	delivering	delivered
15 • occur	occurring	occurred
16 • enter	entering	entered

Non-Progressive Verbs

The verbs below are generally not used in the progressive tense because they indicate an ongoing state rather than a temporary action.

PREFERENCE		A STATE OF BEING		POSSESSION	PERCEPTION
admire	like	agree	notice	belong	appear
appreciate	love	believe	realize	have *	hear
care	mind	consist	recognize	own	imagine
desire	need	cost	refuse	possess	notice
despise	prefer	doubt	remember		see
envy	want	forget	think *		seem
hate		know	trust		smell *
		mean	understand		sound
					taste *
					weigh *

* Some verbs have more than one meaning and can be used in the progressive tense.
  Compare the following pairs of sentences.

Progressive	**Non-Progressive**	
He **is having** a bad day.	He **has** two Picassos.	(Expresses possession)
I **am thinking** about it.	I **think** it is expensive.	(Expresses an opinion)
Why **are** you **smelling** my sock?	My socks **smell** clean.	(Expresses a perception)

EXERCISE 6 > Write the correct form of the verbs in parentheses. Use the present and past tenses.

Example: An extremist (shoot) _____*shot*_____ Mahatma Gandhi in 1948.

1 • What (happen) _____*happened*_____ in the world these days? I (refer) _____*refer*_____ to the violence in the world. I (understand, not) _____*don't understand*_____ it. At this moment, humans (hurt) _____*hurt*_____ each other in every country on the planet. Some people (believe) _____*believe*_____ that aggression should be met with passive resistance.

2 • Many years ago, one man became famous for his belief in non-violence. In 1893, while Mohandas Gandhi (live) _____*lived*_____ in Durban, South Africa, an event changed his life. While he (ride) _____*rode*_____ in a train, another passenger (make) _____*made*_____ a complaint. The stranger (want, not) _____*didn't want*_____ to share the train car with a non-white. Gandhi (refuse) _____*refused*_____ to move to another train car. While he (sit) _____*sat*_____ quietly, a police officer (question) _____*questioned*_____ him. Then the officer (throw) _____*threw*_____ Gandhi's luggage out of the train and attacked him. The event was a turning point in Gandhi's life. He (be) _____*was*_____ upset about discrimination based on race or caste. He (develop) _____*developped*_____ his theory of passive resistance at that time.

3 • Later, when Gandhi (return) _____*returned*_____ to India, he (ask) _____*asked*_____ his followers to resist the British rulers by making peaceful strikes and protests. In 1947, the British (leave) _____*left*_____ India. Today, many people (remember) _____*remembered*_____ the frail man who wanted a non-violent world.

Tip

Common Errors with Progressive Forms
Don't overuse the progressive tense. For example, never use the past progressive tense to talk about past habits or a series of past actions.

                              drew
PAST HABIT   Picasso ~~was drawing~~ pictures of his friends when he was younger.

                                     painted   studied
SERIES OF PAST ACTIONS   When he was young, he ~~was painting~~ pictures, he ~~was studying~~
                         learned
music, and he ~~was learning~~ a second language.

EXERCISE 7 ❯ Underline and correct the errors in the sentences below. Write *C* beside the sentences that are correct.

Example: On that night in 1536, while Anne was ~~sleep~~ *sleeping*, she had a terrible dream.

1 • In 1509, King Henry VIII ~~was becoming~~ *became* the king of England.

C **2** • What Henry was wearing when he married his first wife?

3 • How many women *did* he married?

4 • Eventually the King ~~was marrying~~ *married* six women.

5 • Why were the Royal women of Europe ~~were~~ reluctant to marry Henry?

C **6** • The King's men beheaded two of Henry's wives: Anne Boleyn and her first cousin, Katherine Howard.

7 • Henry ~~was ruling~~ *ruled* England for many years.

King Henry VIII

8 • Today, England still ~~is having~~ *have* a monarchy.

C **9** • Why are many anti-monarchists demonstrating in Hyde Park right now?

10 • They ~~are not believing~~ *don't believe* that the public should pay taxes to support the monarchy.

Subject Questions

When *who, what, how much,* and *how many* ask about the **subject** of a question, no auxiliary is needed.

Lena lives with Jonas.	**Her house** had blue walls.	**Fifty** paintings survived.
Who lives with Jonas?	**What** had blue walls?	**How many paintings** survived?

When *who(m)*, what, how much,* and *how many* ask about the **object** of a question, you must add an auxiliary to the question.

Lena lives with **Jonas**.	Her house had **blue walls**.	She had **fifty** paintings.
Who(m) <u>does</u> Lena live with?	**What** <u>did</u> her house have?	**How many paintings** <u>did</u> she have?

* *Whom* is used in formal and academic English. In informal English, it is acceptable to use *who*.

EXERCISE 8 ❯ Write questions for the sentences below. The answers to the questions are in bold.

Example: **The Berlin Wall** divided a city.   What ___*divided a city?*___

1 • **The oldest human** lives in Germany.   Who *lives in Germany?*

2 • **The incident** happened in 1989.   What *happened in 1989*

3 • Jonas watched **the Berlin Wall fall.**   What _did Jonas watched?_

4 • **The wall** fell on November 9.   What _fell on November 9?_

5 • Jonas celebrated with **his wife Lena.**   Whom _does Jonas celebrated with?_

6 • **Many people** kept pieces of the wall.   Who _kept pieces of the wall?_

 Class Exercise

Twenty Questions
To prepare, think of a very important event in history. You can choose one of the events from the Warm Up on pages 67 and 68 in *Open Road English Skills*, or you can think of a different event. You may need to do some research to find the exact date of the event.

Then, working with a student or team, ask yes/no questions to determine what their moment in time was. Other team members will ask you questions about your event.

Example: Did the event occur in the twentieth century?   Yes
Does it involve a political figure?   No
Is it about a scientific discovery?   Yes

The Future Tenses

TENSE	MEANING	EXAMPLE
Will	• prediction • spontaneous action or gesture of willingness	It **will rain** tomorrow. I'**ll pay** for the meal. She'**ll do** it!
Be going to	• prediction • previously planned action	It **is going to rain** soon. I'**m going to leave**.
The simple present	• schedules	The train **leaves** at noon.
The present progressive	• previously planned event that will happen in the near future	We'**re leaving** tonight. The bus **is leaving** in ten minutes.

Tip

Question and Negative Forms
Review the question and negative forms of *will* and *be going to.*

	Question	**Negative**
Will	Will she arrive soon?	No, she won't arrive soon.
Be going to	Are you going to leave?	No, I'm not going to leave.

EXERCISE 9 ❯ Write the appropriate form of the verbs in parentheses. Note that in some instances, there is more than one possible answer.

Example: If you are having problems, I (help) _____will help_____ you.

1 • Mike: In the election, who (you, vote) _are you going to vote_ for?

2 • Anna: I'm not sure. Maybe I (support) _will support_ the left-leaning candidate. On the other hand, she (raise) _is going to raise_ taxes. At least, she said she would in her campaign literature.

3 • Mike: Perhaps we need higher taxes. How (we, pay) _will we pay_ for rising health care costs?

4 • Anna: Please don't try to influence me. Maybe I just (vote, not) _am not going to vote_. My vote probably (make, not) _won't make_ a difference anyway.

5 • Mike: Don't think that way. Listen, I (watch) _am going to watch_ the debate tonight. Why don't you watch it with me?

6 • Anna: I can't. My train (leave) _is going to leave_ in a few minutes.

7 • Mike: Your train left ten minutes ago! Wait here while I get my keys. I (drive) _will drive_ you home.

Time Clauses

In sentences that indicate the future, use the present tense in time clauses. A time clause begins with any of the following time markers:

after	as soon as	in case	until	when
as long as	before	unless	whatever	whenever

The time marker can appear in the first or second part of the sentence.

Gustavo **will move** to Veracruz **when** he **finishes** university.
      future   time marker + present tense

As soon as he **has** his degree, he **will look** for work in his field.
time marker + present tense   future

> **Tip**
>
> **Never Write _Gonna_**
> Although people say _gonna_, it isn't a proper word. Always write _going to_.
>
>   going to
> I'm ~~gonna~~ finish this project.

Underline the time markers in the sentences below. Then identify and correct the verb errors.

Example: I will leave <u>as soon as</u> I ~~will finish~~ _finish_ my work.

1 • <u>When</u> next winter ~~will arrive~~ _arrive_, will there be a lot of ice rain?

2 • <u>Tomorrow,</u> the highways ~~will become~~ _are going to be_ very slippery after the ice rain will fall.

3 • <u>As soon as</u> the sea levels ~~will rise~~ _rise_, there will be a lot of flooding.

4 • Other problems will occur <u>unless</u> nations ~~will reduce~~ _reduce_ greenhouse gases.

5 • <u>After</u> the election ~~will pass,~~ _pass_ will the situation change?

Part B
Underline and correct five errors involving future tenses.

6 • What are future automobiles <u>gonna</u> _going to_ look like? How large ~~will~~ _are_ they going to be? Will the future car ~~will~~ be as small as a motorcycle? As soon as car companies ~~will~~ _are going to_ develop alternative fuel sources, consumers will no longer be dependent on gasoline. Some vehicles run on solar power, cooking oil, electricity, and vegetable waste. However, unless oil companies and governments ~~will~~ actively promote alternative fuels, consumers will not be able to buy such vehicles.

Avoiding Double Negatives

A double negative occurs when you combine a negative word such as _no_, _nothing_, _nobody_, or _nowhere_, with a negative adverb such as _not_, _never_, _rarely_, or _seldom_. The result is a sentence that has a doubly negative meaning. Such sentences can be confusing because the negative words cancel each other out.

Double Negative: She <u>doesn't</u> give <u>no</u> interviews.

There are several ways to correct double negatives. Either remove one of the two negative forms, or change _no_ to _any_.

Double Negative	**Possible Corrections**
She **doesn't** have no money.	She doesn't have money. (Remove _no_.)
	She has no money. (Remove _doesn't_.)
	She doesn't have any money. (Change _no_ to _any_.)

When to Use the Base Form
Use the base form of verbs that follow the auxiliaries *do*, *does*, and *did*. Also, use the base form in infinitives (*to* + the base form).

change	talk

Did he <u>changed</u> his mind? Did he offer to <u>talked</u> about the issue?

EXERCISE 11 Underline and correct the errors in the sentences below. If the sentence is correct, write *C* in the space provided.

Example: Did you <u>heard</u> about the origins of Medicare? _____ *hear* _____

1 • What will you do when you will have a medical problem? _____ *are going to* _____

2 • During Canada's first decades, most people didn't <u>have no</u> health care. _____ *have any health* _____

3 • What <u>did happen</u> in 1947? _____ *happened* _____

4 • The premier of Saskatchewan wanted to removed the burden of medical expenses from families. _____ *C* _____

5 • In 1947, Premier Tommy Douglas signed into law the first universal health care program in North America. _____ *C* _____

6 • Why did some doctors disliked the program? _____ *C* _____

7 • Doctors didn't want no government officials to control their salaries. _____ *C* _____

8 • When did universal health care <u>arrived</u> in every province? _____ *arrive* _____

9 • It wasn't until 1972 that all provinces <u>were</u> agreeing to have the Medicare system. _____ *agreed* _____

10 • When the new budget <u>will pass</u>, our province will hire more doctors. _____ *is going to pass* _____

❯ Take Another Look

Answer the following questions. If you don't know an answer, go back and review the appropriate section.

1 • Underline and correct the errors in the sentences below. Then explain why the sentences are incorrect.

Example: Every day, he <u>is complaining</u> about something. _____ *complains* _____
Rule: *Don't use the present progressive with habitual actions.*

a) Last year, I was working every weekend. _____ *worked* _____

Rule: _____

b) Did you learned a second language? _____learn_____

Rule: _____

c) Vince wanted to talked with you. _____talk_____

Rule: _____

d) He will arrive when he will finish work. _____finishes_____

Rule: _____

e) We don't need no education. _____any_____

Rule: _____

2• Write the past form of the following verbs.

Example: bring ____*brought*____

a) fall ____fell____   **c)** teach ____thought____

b) sing ____rang____   **d)** think ____thought____

Final Review

Part A

Write the correct form of each verb in parentheses. Use the past, present, or future tenses.

Example: Some inventions (cause) ____*cause*____ unexpected problems.

1• What jobs (be) ____are____ dangerous? Why (people, do) ____people do____ hazardous jobs? When you (graduate) ____are going to graduate____ from college, will you work with hazardous materials?

2• In 1898, Marie Curie discovered radium and polonium. Why (her discovery, start) ____did it start____ a radium craze? In the early 1900s, people liked the blue glow of radium and added the substance to clocks and watches. At that time, most people (know, not) ____didn't know____ about the dangers of radium. They (be, not) ____weren't____ careful with the product.

3• In 1917, Grace Fryer worked for the United States Radium Company. The factory owners (explain, not) ____didn't explain____ that radium may be unsafe even though they knew the truth. One day, while Grace (paint) ____was painting____ watch faces with radium, she suddenly (feel) ____felt____ very sick. In the following months, her teeth (fall) ____fell____ out. Doctors discovered that she had advanced bone decay in her mouth and spine.

Part B
Underline and correct five errors with verb tense or double negatives.

take
Example: The girls didn't <u>took</u> precautions.

4 • Grace's coworkers didn't know <u>nothing</u> *any* about the dangers of radium. Sometimes they were licking their paintbrushes to make the ends pointy. In 1922, Grace and four other workers filed a lawsuit against U.S. Radium. The "Radium Girls," who were all sick, <u>were wanting</u> *wanted* $250,000 each in compensation. A Federal Court judge asked the desperate women to accept an out-of-court settlement.

5 • Today U.S. Radium doesn't exist <u>no</u> *any* more. In the future, when people <s>will</s> *are going to* work with radium, they <u>will</u> *are going to* have to wear special protective clothing.

Part C
Write questions for the sentences below. The answers to the questions are in bold.
Example: He is talking about **Marie Curie**. *Who is he talking about?*

6 • Curie won the Nobel Prize **because she did ground-breaking work in physics.**
   Why did Curie win the Nobel Prize

7 • She **was eating** when she heard the news.
   What was she doing when she heard the news.

8 • The director is going to make a film about **Curie's life**.
   What is the director going to make a film about?

9 • He makes movies **with his wife.**
   With who does he make movies?

10 • They are discussing **radium** right now.
   What are they discussing right now?

Wrap Up

Specific Verbs
With a partner, brainstorm ten verbs that describe very specific actions. Examples of specific verbs are *whimper, sniffle, slurp,* or *wrestle.* You can use your dictionary to come up with good verbs. Try to find verbs that are very vivid and unusual.

After you have completed your list, exchange sheets with another team. Using the other team's sheet, you and your partner must write a paragraph incorporating the ten verbs.

Present Perfect Tenses

The Present Perfect Tense

A past participle combines with *have* or *has* to form the **present perfect** tense. You can use this tense in two different circumstances.

1 • Use the present perfect to show that an action began in the past and continues to the present.

Key words: since, for, ever, not yet, so far, up to now, recently

2001
I watched my first
James Bond movie.

NOW

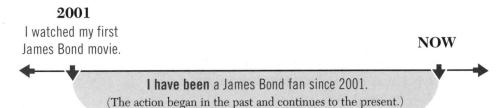

I have been a James Bond fan since 2001.
(The action began in the past and continues to the present.)

2 • Use the present perfect to show that one or more completed actions occurred at unimportant or unspecified times in the past.

Key words: already, once, twice, several times, many times

PAST   **NOW**

(The viewings occurred at unspecified times in the past.)

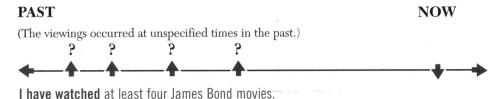

I have watched at least four James Bond movies.

Present Perfect Forms

Form	I You We They } **have** + past participle (met, seen, etc.)	He She It } **has** + past participle (gone, had, etc.)
Question	Move the auxiliary (*have* or *has*) before the subject. **Have** you ever met Donald? **Has** Joe been to China?	
Negative	Put *not* after *have* or *has*. I have **not** (haven't) met Donald. Joe has **not** (hasn't) been to China.	

Class Exercise

Answer the following questions in complete sentences.

1 • Where do you live?

2 • How long have you lived there?

3 • Who is your best friend?

4 • When did you first meet him or her?

5 • How long have you known your best friend?

6 • Do you like funny movies?

7 • What funny movies have you seen?

8 • Have you been to another country?

9 • What countries have you visited?

10 • When did you last visit another country?

Tip

Use the Past Participle

When you write a verb in the present perfect, use the past participle after *have* or *has*. See Appendix 1 for a list of irregular past participles.

        acted   met
She has ~~act~~ in many films, and she has ~~meet~~ many directors.

EXERCISE 1 ❯ Underline eight present perfect verbs. Then correct past-participle errors in six of those verbs.

                                  learned

Example: Those acting students <u>have learn</u> the Stanislavski method.

1 • Many people have <u>thought</u> about becoming famous actors. Acting seems like an
                         spent
easy thing to do; however, most successful actors <u>have spend</u> years developing
their craft.

                           discovered

2 • Some famous actors <u>have discover</u> that fame can end as quickly as it begins. For
example, <u>have you ever heard</u> of Winona Ryder? <u>Have you saw her</u> in any movies
          appeared   *acted*
lately? She <u>has appear</u> in very successful films. She <u>has acted</u> in dramas, comedies,
and thrillers. She was tremendously famous in the early 1990s and as quickly as her
                                    taught
flame rose, it burned out. Her experiences <u>have teached</u> others to appreciate fame
while it lasts.

Tip

When the Main Verb Is *Have*

When the main verb is *have*, you must add the auxiliary *have* or *has* to form the present perfect.

My sister **has had** many health problems. We **have had** many family meetings.

EXERCISE 2 ❯ Fill in the blanks using the tenses indicated.

Part A
Simple past — The action was over at a known past time.

Example: World War II (begin) with the Nazi invasion of Poland in 1939. _____ *began* _____

1 • On August 6, 1945, a Boeing B-29 bomber (fly) over Hiroshima. _____ flew _____

2 • The bomber (drop) an atomic bomb called "Little Boy." _____ dropped _____

3 • Three days later, a bomb called "Fat Boy" (fall) on Nagasaki. _____ fell _____

4 • The bombs (destroy) those two cities. _____ destroyed _____

Part B
Present perfect — The action began in the past and continues to the present.

Example: Over fifty years (pass) since the Hiroshima bombing. _____ *have passed* _____

5 • Since 1945, some scientists (try) to develop better bombs. _____ have tried _____

6 • For fifty years, many nations (invest) in nuclear arms. _____ have invested _____

7 • India (have) nuclear weapons since 1974. _____ have had _____

8 • Since 1980, both the United States and Russia (promise) to reduce their nuclear arsenals. _____ have promised _____

Part C
Present perfect — The actions occurred at unknown past times.

Example: There (be) many wars in Asia. _____ *have been* _____

9 • Hiroshima citizens (rebuild, already) their city. _____ have already rebuilded _____

10 • I (visit) Hiroshima three times. _____ have visit _____

11 • Many Hollywood directors (make) movies about the war years. _____ have made _____

12 • Stephen Spielberg (direct) at least two war movies. _____ have directed _____

Lie Detector
Write two sentences about yourself—one that is about something you have really done and the other about something that you haven't done. Do not indicate which sentence is a lie.

> **Example:** I have eaten shark meat. (true)
> I have travelled to Brazil. (false)

Work with a partner. Show the sentences to your partner. You must pretend that both sentences are true. Your partner will ask you questions to discover which sentence is a lie. Invent answers for the false story.

Tip

Looking at Key Words
Use key words to help you decide what tense to use. Be careful: when the past time is stated and other sentences give details about that past time, use the past tense.

> Nantha **has been** a set designer **since** he graduated from college. Four years **ago**, he **moved** to England. He **stayed** in a small hotel in London, and he **went** to several plays.

EXERCISE 3 > **Part A**

Complete the following sentences with the past or present perfect tense. Underline the key words or phrases that indicate why the tense should be used.

> **Example:** We (learn) _____*have learned*_____ a lot <u>since</u> we started school.

1• Eighty years ago, the special effects in movies (be) _____were_____ amazing. For example, in 1934, set designers (construct) _____have constructed_____ miniature sky scrapers and model airplanes for the movie *King Kong*. Artists (create) _____have created_____ a model of the giant ape and then (move) _____moved_____ it slightly every few frames of film.

2• Since 1934, audiences (see) _____have seen_____ many special effects. Since the 1980s, computerized techniques (become) _____has become_____ quite sophisticated. For over ten years, artists (work) _____have worked_____ with computer animation. For example, in 1995, *Toy Story* (be) _____has been_____ the first completely computer-animated film. Since then, many other computer-animated films (hit) _____have hitted_____ movie screens.

3 • Kevin Auclair (be) _has been_ a makeup artist for fifteen years. Theatrical makeup (improve) _has improved_ a lot since Kevin's career began. He (use) _has used_ latex to create a variety of interesting effects for more than eight years. In the 2001 film *The Lord of the Rings*, the hobbits (wear) _have wore_ large latex feet and ears.

Part B

Answer the following questions about the paragraphs in Part A.

4 • What tense is used with the word *ago*? _simple past_

5 • Why is the simple past tense used in Paragraph 1? _____

_____

6 • Write down the words or phrases that follow the word *since* in Part A: _1934_ _audiences have seen many special effects_

7 • Write down the phrases that follow the word *for* in Part A: _Over ten years, artists have worked with computer animation_

8 • Complete the following rules. Write *since*, *for*, or *ago* in the spaces provided.

Ago refers to a past time when the action was completed.

Example: I moved here three months _ago_.

Since refers to a specific past moment when the action began. The action continues to the present time.

Example: I've been here _since_ March.

For refers to a period of time.

Example: I've been here _for_ three months.

Present Perfect vs. Simple Past

Look at the difference between the simple past and present perfect tenses.

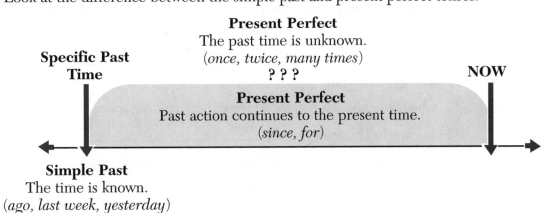

Simple Past: In 1962, Sean Connery <u>appeared</u> in the first James Bond film, *Dr. No.*
(The event occurred at a known past time.)

Present Perfect: James Bond movies <u>have been</u> popular for over forty years.
(The action began in the past and continues to the present.)

Many different actors <u>have played</u> James Bond.
(The repeated past actions have occurred at unspecified past times.)

EXERCISE 4 ❯ Fill in the blanks with the present perfect or the simple past tenses. Then explain why you chose the tense.

Example: Keira (live) with me since March. _____*has lived*_____

Reason: *The action began in the past (March) and continues to the present.*

1 • Marilyn (buy) a new violin two months ago. _____*bought*_____

Reason: *The event occured at a known past time*

2 • She (be) a concert violinist since 1990. _____*has been*_____

Reason: *the action began in the past and continues to the pr.*

3 • Marilyn (perform) in many countries. _____*performed*_____

Reason: *the event ...*

4 • Keira (move) into Marilyn's place three years ago. _____*moved*_____

Reason: *the event ~*

5 • Keira and Marilyn (be) roommates since then. _____*have been*_____

Reason: *the action*

EXERCISE 5 ❯ Fill in the blanks with the present perfect or the simple past tenses.

Example: Many horror movies (become) _____*have become*_____ classics.

1 • Since the 1920s, some of America's most respected actors (appear) _____*have*_____
_____*appeared*_____ in horror movies. For many years, Johnny Depp (choose)
_____ diverse roles, including that of a pirate, a
detective, and an eccentric journalist. However, he (be, also) _____*has also*_____
_____*been*_____ in many horror movies. (you, see, ever) _____*have you*_____
_____*ever seen*_____ *Nightmare on Elm Street?* Depp (appear) _____*appeared*_____
_____ in the original film in 1984.

2 • Brad Pitt (perform, also) _____*has also performed*_____ in several horror
movies. He (be) _____*was*_____ in 1989's *Cutting Class*,
which was about a maniac who went on a killing spree.

3 • Leonardo DiCaprio (work) _____*has worked*_____ as an actor since
he was eleven years old. He (take, also) _____*also took*_____ roles
in several low-budget features. He (act) _____*acted*_____ in

UNIT 3 ·· Present Perfect Tenses © Pearson Longman – Reproduction prohibited the 1991 horror movie, *The Critters*. Clearly, many horror movies (provide) _____have provided_____ today's most popular actors with essential film experience.

Question Words

Have you ever …?
Use this form to determine if something happened at an indefinite past time. Use *never* to specify that something hasn't occurred in a person's life.

Have you **ever** been to Chile? No, I have **never** been there.

How long …?
Use this form to determine the period of time that an action lasted.

How long has Ms. Malone been the mayor? She has been the mayor for twelve years.

How many (times) …?
Use this form to ask about the repetition of an activity.

How many times have you been to Portugal? I have been there twice.

EXERCISE 6 〉 Write questions for the following sentences. The answers to the questions are in bold.

Example: I have **never** sung in public.   *Have you ever sung in public?*

1 • Eric has played in **three** different bands.
   How many different bands has Eric played in?

2 • He has been a drummer **for two years**.
   For how long has he been a drummer?

3 • Elise has **never** played the drums.
   Has Elise played the drums?

4 • They have lived together **since 2002**.
   Since when have they lived together?

5 • They have **never** played music together.
   Have they played music together?

Tip

Present Perfect or Simple Past?
Use the past tense when referring to someone who is no longer living. Only use the present perfect tense when the action has a relationship to someone or something that still exists.

wrote
Chopin ~~has written~~ many great piano compositions.

Don't use the present perfect tense when the past time is known.

moved
Five years ago, Karine ~~has moved~~ to Paris.

EXERCISE 7 ❭ Underline and correct the errors in the sentences below. Write *C* beside the sentences that are correct.

Example: Have you ever <u>saw</u> a magician?   *seen*

1 • Since the beginning of humanity, people are visiting psychics and fortune tellers.   *C*

2 • In 1898, when Harry Houdini turned twenty, he <u>has become</u> famous for his escapes.   *became*

3 • In the years before his death, Houdini became obsessed with exposing fraudulent fortune tellers.   *C*

4 • Since Houdini's death, many subsequent magicians have <u>try</u> to copy his tricks.   *tried*

5 • Very few magicians <u>had have</u> as much success as Houdini.   *have had*

6 • James Myron is a magician since 1991.   *C*

7 • Since Myron's career began, he <u>made</u> many difficult underwater escapes.   *has made*

8 • In 2002, Myron <u>has begun</u> to investigate fraudulent magicians.   *began*

9 • Since then, he <u>have</u> exposed many would-be psychics, mediums, and fortune tellers.   *has*

10 • For example, in 1996, he proved that TV evangelist Peter Upwell was fooling the audience.   *C*

EXERCISE 8 ❭ Fill in the blanks with the correct verb tense. You can use the simple present, the simple past, or the present perfect.

Example: There ___*have been*___ many important historical moments during my lifetime.
(be)

1 • The world ___*has changed*___ a lot throughout history. Different
(change)

political systems ___*have risen*___ and ___*fell*___
(rise)   (fall)

since 1900. In 1917, Soviet idealists ___*attempted*___ to create a society
(attempt)

with no class system, and yet a privileged political class ___*replaced*___
(replace)

the wealthy class during the Communist era. Then, in 1989, the Berlin Wall

___*fell*___ under the weight of protestors.
(fall)

2 • More recently, some countries ___*have seen*___ their standard of living
(see)

change dramatically. For example, in 1988, almost fifty thousand people

___*left*___ Ireland to find work elsewhere. Ireland's economy
(leave)

_____ *has improved* _____ a lot since 1990. Last year, almost twenty
(improve)

thousand people _____ *returned* _____ to Ireland.
(return)

The Present Perfect Progressive Tense

The **present perfect progressive** indicates that an action has been in progress
from a past time up until the present moment. This tense emphasizes the duration
of the uninterrupted activity.

Form: have / has been + <u>verb</u> -*ing*

Samir **has been talking** for twenty minutes. When will he stop talking?

You can also use the present perfect progressive tense to indicate that the results of
an action are still visible.

Somebody **has been sleeping** in my bed. (The sheets are rumpled.)

Somebody **has slept** in my bed. (The event could have happened a month ago.)

With some verbs, such as *live*, *work*, *teach*, and *study*, the present perfect and the
present perfect progressive tenses have essentially the same meaning.

Ian **has been working** here for a week.   Ian **has worked** here for a week.

Class Exercise

Answer the following questions.

1 • Dylan has worked on my car.
   Kelly has been working on my car.
   Who has greasy hands? _____ *Kelly* _____

2 • Alex has ridden his bike for six hours.
   Philippe has been riding his bike for six hours.
   Who is sweaty? _____ *Philippe* _____

3 • Mieko has lived in Newfoundland for seven years.
   Mieko has been living in Newfoundland for seven years.
   Do these sentences have the same meaning? _____ *No* _____

EXERCISE 9 ❭ Fill in the blanks with the present perfect or the present perfect progressive.

1 • Luis and Alicia (be) _____ *have been* _____ to Arizona
several times. Right now, they are returning home to Halifax. Alicia (drive)
_____ *has been driving* _____ for nine hours and she is very
tired. Luis (sleep) _____ *has been sleeping* _____ for three hours.
Alicia (ask) _____ *has asked* _____ Luis several times to drive, but he
(refuse) _____ *has refused* _____ each time. He says that he has a
headache.

2• They are at the border crossing. They (have, never) _have never had_ a problem crossing the border. However, earlier today a guard pulled them over. They (wait) _have been waiting_ for two hours. Border guards (inspect) _have inspected_ their car since three o'clock.

❯ Take Another Look

Answer the following questions. If you don't know an answer, go back and review the appropriate section.

1• When do you use the present perfect tense? Give two explanations.

a) _____

b) _____

2• Fill in the blanks with *since* or *for*.

a) _Since_ last April

b) _Since_ a month

c) _Since_ a particular past time

d) _For_ a few weeks

e) _Since_ I graduated

f) _For_ a period of time

3• Underline and correct the errors in the following sentences. Then write a rule to explain your correction.

a) Robert Ludlum ~~has~~ published his first
book in 1971.   _____

Reason: _the event occurred at a known past time_

b) He has wrote twenty-one spy novels.   _____

Reason: _____

c) Ludlum is a well-known author <u>for</u> over   _since_
thirty years.

Reason: _____

d) Millions of people <u>bought</u> his novel,   _have bought_
The Bourne Identity.

Reason: _the action happened and continues_

Final Review ➤

Part A

Fill in the blanks with the simple past or present perfect form of the verbs in parentheses.

Example: For the last six years, my cousin Mike (be) _has been_ a James Bond fanatic.

1• Spy fans around the world (watch) _have watched_ James Bond movies since the mid-1960s. Many different actors (play) _played_ _____ the role of Bond. Although most people have heard of James Bond, few people know about the man behind the movies—Ian Fleming.

2· Ian Fleming (live) _____lived_____ from 1906 to 1964. During his childhood, his father (be) _____was_____ a successful stockbroker. As a result, Ian (spend) _____has spent_____ his youth living a high-class lifestyle. In the 1940s, the British Secret Service (draft) _____drafted_____ Ian Fleming because he could easily mix with high-society officials. For several years during the 1940s, he (be) _____has been_____ a spy.

3· In 1953, Fleming (use) _____used_____ his experiences to create his first James Bond book. Since then, James Bond (be) _____has become_____ extremely popular. For over forty years, viewers around the world (see) _____have seen_____ the sophisticated spy in action.

4· Since the first film, the James Bond character (age, never) _____has never aged_____. For more than forty years, beautiful women (try) _____have tried_____ to seduce him, and villains (want) _____have wanted_____ to kill him.

5· Over and over, Bond (escape) _____has escaped_____ danger by using his intelligence, his fast cars, and his secret weapons. Since its debut, the James Bond character (capture) _____has captured_____ the audience's imagination.

>>> Sean Connery as James Bond

Part B

Underline and correct the errors involving verb tense.
Write *C* beside the sentences that are correct.

6· Since the 1950s, many actresses ~~were~~ have been the "Bond girl."

7· For example, Halle Berry ~~has been~~ was Bond's adversary and lover in the 2002 film *Die Another Day*.

8· For the past twenty years, some women have complain about the secondary role of females in the Bond films. C

9· However, according to James Bond supporters, the Bond character is a harmless fantasy since its creation. C

10· Have you ever ~~saw~~ seen a James Bond movie?

 **Wrap Up**

Tell the Truth

Join a team of two or three other students and talk about interesting or unusual things that you have done. For example, have you ever

- been to an exciting or interesting place?
- won an award, a competition, or a contest?
- hurt yourself or had an accident?
- met a famous person?
- lost something important?
- gotten lost?
- witnessed a crime?

Choose one story for your team. The story must be true for one person and a complete lie for the others in the group. After arriving in front of the class, all of you must make the same statement. When students ask you questions, one will tell the truth and the others will lie. Your classmates must guess who is telling the truth.

For example, Pedro, Alex, and Kim are in a team. Last year, Pedro won $5,000 in a lottery. All three students say, "I have won money in a lottery."

When the students in the class ask questions, Pedro, Kim, and Alex can give different details about their stories. For instance, Kim can say that she has won $5,000, and Alex can say that he has won $200, as long as everyone sticks to the essential story of "I have won money in a lottery."

Past and Future Perfect Tenses

The Past Perfect Tense

The past perfect tense indicates that one past action happened before another past action.

The movie started.　　　Rene arrived.　　　　　　　**NOW**

The movie **had started** when Rene arrived.
(past perfect)

Key words: already, up to that time, by then

Past Perfect Forms

Form	**had** + past participle
Question	Move the auxiliary (*had*) before the subject.　What had she done before you arrived?
Negative	Add *not*.　I had **not** (hadn't) eaten when the restaurant closed.

Note: Sometimes, when *before* or *after* is used in a sentence, the past perfect is not necessary because the time relationship is already clear.

For example:　　　　　　The movie **had ended**, so I left the theatre.

You could also write:　　After the movie **ended**, I left the theatre.

 Class Exercise

Can you identify the differences between the simple past and the past perfect tenses? Answer the following questions.

1 • Last night at 9 p.m., Rick had taken the dog for a walk.

　Last night at 9 p.m., Karen took the dog for a walk.

　Whose dog went for a walk before 9 p.m.?　*Rick's dog*

2 • When the second robbery occurred, the police put Mickey in jail.

　When the second robbery occurred, the police had just put Jimmy in jail.

　Who could not have committed the second robbery?　*Jimmy*

3 • When Simon got to the 2004 Olympics, he had won a gold medal.

　When Nicolas got to the 2004 Olympics, he won a gold medal.

　Who was already a gold medal winner before he got to the 2004 Olympics?　*Simon*

EXERCISE 1 > Underline the correct verb tense in parentheses.

Example: When Charlie Chaplin left England, he (already acted / <u>had already acted</u>) in many productions.

1 • Charles Spencer Chaplin was born in a London slum on April 16, 1889, and then, in 1910, he (<u>arrived</u> / had arrived) in America.

2 • Because Chaplin (accumulated / <u>had accumulated</u>) a lot of acting experience in England, he easily found work in Hollywood.

3 • In 1920, Chaplin earned $10,000 per week, which was more than he (ever earned / <u>had ever earned</u>) in his life!

4 • That year, Chaplin (<u>developed</u> / had developed) the "tramp" character, which was inspired by the poverty that he (experienced / <u>had experienced</u>).

5 • When he turned twenty-six years old, he fulfilled a dream that he (had / <u>had had</u>) for several years.

6 • Chaplin (<u>acted</u> / had acted) and (<u>directed</u> / had directed) in his own movies, and in his films, he expressed sympathy for the poor.

7 • FBI agents investigated Chaplin because they thought that he (joined / <u>had joined</u>) the Communist party.

8 • At that time, Chaplin didn't have American citizenship even though he (spent / <u>had spent</u>) most of his professional life in the United States.

9 • In 1952, the U.S. immigration authorities revoked Chaplin's re-entry permit after he (sailed / <u>had sailed</u>) for England.

10 • Although Chaplin (made / <u>had made</u>) many successful American comedies, he (<u>spent</u> / had spent) most of the next years living in exile.

11 • In 1972, Chaplin (<u>returned</u> / had returned) to America to accept a Lifetime Achievement Academy Award.

12 • When Chaplin passed away in 1977, his children knew that he (lived / <u>had lived</u>) an extremely full and rewarding life.

>>> Charlie Chaplin as "the tramp"

EXERCISE 2 › Underline and correct eight errors involving verb tense.

described
Example: They spoke with a journalist, and they <u>had described</u> the UFO.

1• On June 24, 1947, Kenneth Arnold was piloting his plane when he saw what
appeared to be a shiny object in the sky. He was *kept* <u>keeping</u> the object in sight for
about three minutes. He then flew to an FBI office to report what he *had seen* <u>saw</u>. The FBI
office wasn't open, so he *went* had <u>gone</u> to an Oregon-based newspaper office instead.

2• Journalist Bill Bequette was *listened* <u>listening</u> to Arnold's story, and then he produced a
report for the Associated Press. More journalists came and asked Arnold to
describe what he *had witnessed* <u>witnessed</u> in detail.

3• That week in 1947, Arnold's description of a "crescent-shaped" object <u>had appeared</u>
in over one hundred newspapers. That July, more people came forward and claimed
that they *had observed* <u>observed</u> similar flying saucers on June 24. Since 1947, UFO sightings
has <u>increased</u> dramatically.

The Past Perfect Progressive Tense

Use the past perfect progressive to indicate that an action was in progress (without
interruption) before another past action occurred.

When I returned home, I realized that somebody **had been using** my computer. It was still warm.

```
                              I arrived.                    NOW
◄─────────────────────────────────▼─────────────────────▼──────────►
        Somebody had been using my computer
                   before I arrived.
```

EXERCISE 3 › Fill in the blanks with the simple past, the past perfect, or the past perfect progressive.

Example: World War II (begin) _____*began*_____ in 1939 when Germany invaded Poland.
Germany (prepare) _*had been preparing*_ to invade Poland for many months.

1• On August 6, 1939, Canadian soldiers (enter) __*entered*_____
World War II. The United States (declare) __*declared*_____
war on Japan in 1941. Canadian soldiers (fight) _*had fought*_____
for two years when the Americans entered the war.

2• On December 7, 1941, Japanese airplanes (fly) __*flew*_____
over Hawaii. The soldiers on the ground were not worried because no one

(attack, ever) _had ever attacked_ Hawaii before. The first

bomb (shock) _shocked_ the soldiers. Most of the

soldiers (sleep) _had slept_ for about an hour when

the first bomb fell and awakened them.

3. After the war, my great uncle returned home. My great grandparents were

surprised because their son (write, not) _haven't wrote_

for a long time. For several months they (wait) _have waited_

_____ for news when their son suddenly appeared at their door.

The Future Perfect Tense

Use the future perfect tense to indicate that an action will occur before or up to the time of a future action.

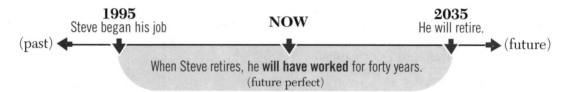

1995
Steve began his job

NOW

2035
He will retire.

(past) ← → (future)

When Steve retires, he **will have worked** for forty years.
(future perfect)

Key words: by the time I retire, by next year, by then, by Monday, by the weekend ...

Future Perfect Forms

Form	**will have** + past participle
Question	Move the auxiliary (*will*) before the subject. How long **will** she **have worked**?
Negative	Add *not*. By next summer, I **will not (won't) have finished** my degree.
Progressive	In the future perfect progressive, use *will have been* + the *-ing* verb form. When I retire, I **will have been working** for forty years.

Tip

Future Progressive and Future Perfect Progressive
Use the future progressive to indicate that an action will be in progress at a future time.
The future perfect progressive shows that an action will be in progress <u>up to</u> a future time.

When you call me tomorrow, I **will be working**. By Sunday, I **will have been working** for thirty hours on this project.

Answer the following questions.

1 • When the exam starts, Trang will still be studying.
   When the exam starts, Fatima will have studied.
   Who will be ready for the exam? _Fatima_

2 • Next Sunday at 1 p.m., Nadine will be finishing her work.
   Next Sunday at 1 p.m., Carolyn will have finished her work.
   Who will relax next Sunday afternoon? _Carolyn_

EXERCISE 4 ❭ Fill in the blanks with the future perfect, the future progressive, or the future perfect progressive.

   Example: Tomorrow, at 9 p.m., don't disturb me because I _will be studying_.
   By next Tuesday, I (spend) _will have spent_ three weeks preparing for the test.

1 • When I finish school next June, I (be) _will have been_ a student for eighteen years.

2 • I work until 10:30 p.m., but my sister's bus arrives at 10 p.m. Tonight, when I enter the station at 10:40 p.m., my sister's bus (arrive) _will have arrived_ and she (wait) _will have waited_ for me for about half an hour.

3 • We have a huge project to do. It is 5 p.m., but we must finish it. Tonight at midnight, we (still, work) _will still be working_ on it. We hope that we will finish on Sunday. By the time we finish the project, we (spend) _will have spent_ over eighty hours on it.

4 • This Academy Awards show is so long. By the time it ends, the show (be) _will have been_ on for four hours!

5 • Don't call me tonight. I'm planning to go to bed at 9 p.m. If you call at 10 p.m., I (sleep) _will be sleeping_.

❭ Take Another Look

Answer the following questions. If you don't know an answer, go back and review the appropriate section.

1 • Underline the past perfect verbs.

were sleeping	had visited	have done	has seen
had tried	has gone	was	had done

2• Underline and correct one error involving verb tenses in each sentence.

a) When I ~~arrived~~ *will* at the party, my hosts had already finish dinner.

b) Why *have they* they had already eaten?

c) I left the party and went to Maria's, but when I arrived at her house, she ~~had~~ went out.

d) Tonight, by the time I go to bed, I will ~~be~~ *have been* awake for twenty hours.

Final Review

Fill in the blanks with the appropriate verb tenses. You can use any form of the present, past, or future tenses.

Example: In past centuries, kings and queens (have) _____ *had* _____ tremendous power.

1• These days in our history class, we (learn) _____ *learned* _____ about ancient Egypt. So far, we (have) _____ *have had* _____ six quizzes. Tomorrow, when I (arrive) _____ *will arrive* _____ in class, my professor will give us a two-hour exam on ancient Egypt.

2• In 55 BC, when the king of Egypt (die) _____ *died* _____, the Egyptian people (expect) _____ *have expected* _____ his death for many months. The king's seventeen-year-old daughter, Cleopatra, (become) _____ *became* _____ the queen of Egypt, and she (marry) _____ *married* _____ her brother, Ptolemy, according to ancient tradition.

3• Three years later, when Julius Caesar (enter) _____ *entered* _____ Egypt, Ptolemy arranged a visit with the Roman ruler, but he excluded his sister. Cleopatra wanted to be a part of any deals, so she (plan) _____ *had planned* _____ to meet Caesar too. She (hide) _____ *hide* _____ inside a rug and was delivered to Caesar's room.

>>> Queen Cleopatra and a servant

4 • Cleopatra (seduce) ___seduced___ Caesar. He told Cleopatra that he (see, never) ___has never seen___ such a beautiful woman. When he first (hear) ___heard___ her sing, he insisted that he (never, hear) ___had never heard___ such a sweet voice. That night, while the couple (whisper) ___whispered___ in bed, Cleopatra (convince) ___convinced___ Caesar to make her the sole ruler of Egypt.

5 • The next morning, Ptolemy arrived in Caesar's room and (realize) ___realized___ that Cleopatra (meet, already) ___had already met___ the foreign ruler. Ptolemy was furious and he (shout) ___shouted___ that his wife (spend) ___had spent___ the night with another man. Ptolemy then (threaten) ___threated___ Caesar with revenge. In retaliation, Caesar (order) ___ordered___ Ptolemy's death. By the time Cleopatra and Caesar sailed for Rome, some guards (kill) ___had killed___ Ptolemy.

6 • I (learn) ___have learned___ a lot about ancient Egypt since my course began. By the time we have our test tomorrow, I (study) ___will have studied___ for about twenty hours!

Wrap Up

Reflections
Work with a partner. Take turns completing the next sentences. Try to speak without stopping, and brainstorm as many ideas as possible.

By the time I entered primary school, I had learned …

By the time I finished high school, I had learned …

By the time I finish college, I will have learned …

Example: By the time I entered primary school, I had learned to tie my shoes. I had also learned to share. I had not yet learned to be a good loser.

Modal Auxiliaries

When you place a modal before a verb, it adds a different meaning to the verb. For example, in the sentence *I can read*, the word *can* indicates ability.

Here is a list of common modals. Review the present and past forms.

Modal Forms

FUNCTION	MODAL	EXAMPLE	PAST FORM
Ability	**can**	She **can speak** English.	She **could speak** Greek when she was young.
Offers Requests	**may** **would** **could** **can**	**May** I **help** you? (formal) **Would** you **like** some tea? **Could** you **pass** the butter? **Can** I **have** some help? (informal)	
Advice	**should** **ought to**	Alan **should see** a lawyer. Karen **ought to do** her work.	He **should have seen** a lawyer. She **ought to have done** it.
Necessity	**must** **have to** *	Jason **must work** now. She **has to go** to the hospital.	Jason **had to work** last night. She **had to go** there yesterday.
Probability	**must**	Kay **must be** at home now.	She **must have been** at home.
Possibility	**could** **might** **may**	Dan **could help** you. Mary **might do** the job. Ann **may help** them.	Dan **could have helped** you. Mary **might have done** it. Anne **may have helped** them.
Conditional Desire Past habit	**would**	If I had time, I **would help** her. I **would like** more tea. As a youth, I **would drive** for hours.	I **would have helped** her. I **would have liked** more tea.

* Although *have to* is not a modal auxiliary, it is included on this list because it functions like a modal and has the same meaning as *must*. *Have to* is the only word on the list that requires an *s* in the third-person singular form.

Had Better

You can use the form *had better* to indicate a strong recommendation.

You **had better hurry** or you'll miss the bus.

Shall

The modal *shall* is rarely used in North America. In Britain, *shall* can replace *should* when asking a polite question, as in "Shall I help you?" *Shall* can also be used instead of *will* to indicate a future action, as in "I shall phone you tomorrow."

> **Class Exercise**
>
> Answer the following questions. You can refer to the chart on page 44.
>
> 1 • One of the modals on the chart is actually a regular verb and requires an *s* in the third-person singular form. Which one is it? ___have to___
>
> 2 • Do the other modals need an *s* when the subject is third-person singular? ___No___
>
> 3 • Which two modals indicate advice? ___should___ ___ought to___
>
> 4 • Which two modals indicate necessity? ___must___ ___have to___
>
> 5 • Which three modals indicate possibility? ___could___ ___might___ ___may___
>
> 6 • Read the sentences below and then answer the question that follows.
>   Debra *must get* some rest. Suvendu *has to get* some rest.
>
>   Both of the verb phrases have the same past form. What is it? _____

EXERCISE 1 ▸ Insert modals in the spaces provided. In some cases, there may be more than one answer.

Example: We (*advice*, leave) ___should leave___ now. It's getting late.

1 • Every nation has special restrictions and rules. For example, in China, citizens (*ability*, not, surf) ___can surf___ the Internet freely. Users who type in the word democracy (*possibility*, lose) ___might lose___ their freedom. A Shanghai college student named Wayne (*ability*, speak) ___can speak___ from his own experience. Each time he enters an Internet café, he reads a notice that says, "Users (*advice*, not) ___should not___ break the rules."

2 • Wayne (*possibility*, study) ___may study___ in Canada next year. When he was younger, Wayne (*past ability*, understand, not) ___cannot understand___ English. However, now he studies English every day. He (*necessity*, pass) ___has to pass___ an English placement test before he (*ability*, study) ___can study___ in Vancouver. Wayne (*necessity*, leave) ___must leave___ China soon. He thinks the police (*possibility*, arrest) ___could arrest___ him.

Tip

Must not vs. *Don't Have To*
In negative sentences, *must* and *have to* have different meanings.
You **must not play** with that gun!   It is forbidden.
You **don't have to stay** here. You can leave.   There is no obligation to do it.

EXERCISE 2 ⟩ Fill in the blanks with the negative form of *must* or *have to*.

Example: The children ___*must not*___ touch the dog. He is very fierce.

1 • In Canada, you ___must not___ carry a baby on your lap while driving. It is illegal.

2 • In England, you ___must not___ drive on the right side of the road. The traffic laws are different, and everyone must drive on the left side of the road.

3 • In English pubs, you ___don't have to___ tip the bartender. It isn't expected.

4 • England has strict gun-control laws. You ___must not___ bring a firearm into the country. It is illegal.

5 • Gary ___doesn't have to___ stay in a hotel. If he wants, he can stay with my aunt.

Past Forms
Past Forms of *Must*

Must can indicate an obligation, but it can also mean that something is probable.
• When *must* means "it is necessary," the past form is *had to*.
   She must leave now.   She **had to leave**.
• When *must* means "it is probable," the past form is *must have* + the past participle.
   He must be tired.   He **must have been** tired.

EXERCISE 3 ⟩ Read the following sentences and decide if *must* indicates a probability (*P*) or a necessity (*N*). Then write the past form of the modal.

Example: There **must be** a mouse scratching on the wall. ___*P*___

   Past form: Yesterday, there ___*must have been*___ a mouse scratching on the wall.

1 • Anna's scarf is beautiful. It **must cost** a lot. ___P___

   Past form: The scarf Anna wore last year was beautiful. It ___must had costed___ a lot.

2 • Anna **must use** a respirator. She has damaged lungs. ___N___

   Past form: Last year, Anna ___must had used___ a respirator.

46   UNIT 5 ·· Modal Auxiliaries   © Pearson Longman – Reproduction prohibited

3 • Her snake **must live** in a warm environment or else it will die. _N_

Past form: Her former snake _must have lived_ in a warm environment or else it would die.

4 • She looks terrible. She **must be** very tired. _P_

Past form: Last Friday, she looked terrible. She _must had been_ very tired.

5 • Simon cut himself and he **must get** stitches. _N_

Past form: Yesterday, Simon cut himself and he _must has got_ stitches.

Past Forms of *Should*, *Would*, and *Could*

To form the past tense of modals such as *should, could,* and *would*, add *have* + the past participle.

> Before Anik and Richard went to Mexico, they **should <u>have learned</u>** a few words of Spanish. They **could <u>have communicated</u>** with the locals, and they **would <u>have had</u>** a better time.

EXERCISE 4 Write the past form of the verb phrases in bold.

Example: The doctors **should be more** careful. _should have been_

Present	Past
1 • Ellis Wong **can't read** music.	_cannot red_
2 • He **has to hear** a song before playing it.	
3 • Perhaps he **should study** musical theory.	_should have studied_
4 • He **might need** extra practice.	_might have needed_
5 • You **shouldn't disturb** him.	_shouldn't have disturbed_
6 • He **may join** a punk band.	_may had joined_
7 • His father **can play** the violin.	
8 • Would you **like** to hear him play?	_Have you liked_

EXERCISE 5 Fill in the blanks with the appropriate modal or verb form. Remember to write the correct past form, when necessary.

Example: In the early 1900s, a woman (can, earn, not) _couldn't earn_ a living easily.

1 • Frida Kahlo was born in 1907. She (can, paint) _can paint_ very well. When she was eighteen, she was in a terrible accident and she (have to, stay) _had to stay_ in bed for many months. The handrail from a bus went through her body, so she (must, be) _must had been_ in tremendous pain.

2 • Frida was respected for her art, and even in the 1940s, people (have to, pay) _____have to pay_____ a lot for her paintings. She (must, be) _____must has been_____ very wealthy because she lived in a beautiful house.

3 • Van Gogh was also a famous artist. He (may, paint) _____may have painted_____ over 800 paintings, but many of his works have disappeared. During his lifetime, art patrons (should, appreciate) _____should have appreciated_____ Van Gogh's work, but he was ignored. Today, a Van Gogh painting (can, fetch) _____can fetch_____ several million dollars. A wealthy investor (might, buy) _____might buy_____ one of his self-portraits at an auction next month. My great grandparents (should, buy) _____should have bought_____ a Van Gogh painting many years ago.

Question Forms

Because a modal is an auxiliary, simply move the modal before the subject in question forms.

He can sing.   ❯   **Can** he sing?
She should work harder. ❯   **Should** she work harder?

Exception: *Have To*

Remember that *have to* is actually a regular verb, so you need to add *do*, *does*, or *did* to question forms.

Bruno has to work late. ❯   **Does** Bruno have to work late?

EXERCISE 6 ❯ Write questions for the sentences below. The answers to the questions are in bold.

Example: We should go to **Jamaica** next summer.
Where should we go next summer?

1 • **Yes**, we can visit the birthplace of Bob Marley.
Can we visit ~ ?

2 • We should buy **sunscreen**.
What should we buy?

3 • **Bob Marley** must have had a lot of talent.
Who must have had ... ?

4 • His mother should have known **that Bob would become famous.**
What should his mother have known

5 • Doctors had to operate on Marley **in 1977**.
When did doctors had to ...?

Use Standard Modal Forms

Never Write *Should of* or *Shoulda*

In spoken English, it sounds as if people are saying *should of* or *shoulda*. These are non-standard forms and you should avoid using them. Instead, in the past forms of modals such as *should, could,* or *would,* always include *have* + the past participle.

                         should have
When he did business in Japan, he ~~shoulda~~ learned about Japanese business etiquette.

Never Write *Gotta*

Gotta is not a word and should never be written. It is really an incorrect contraction of *got* and *to*. In formal English, it is preferable to write and say *have to,* for example, "I have to leave." In informal English, you can also say, "I've got to leave."

    have to
I ~~gotta~~ finish this book soon.

EXERCISE 7 Underline and correct twelve errors involving modal forms.

                 should have read
Example: In high school, I <u>shoulda read</u> Chang's novel.

1 • My friend has <u>gotta</u> [got to] choose a novel for her literature class. She can reading any

   book that she wants. I think that she <u>should to</u> read Jung Chang's historical novel

   Wild Swans. In 1992, right after the book came out, a producer <u>shoulda</u> [should have] made the

   book into a movie. Chang's fascinating story describes the lives of her ancestors.

2 • Chang's grandmother, Yu-fang, was born in 1909. Yu's father would <u>of</u> [have] preferred a

   son. When Yu-fang was a child, her toes were broken and her feet were bound

   tightly in cloth, so she can't walk properly. She would have liked to escape such a

   fate, but at that time, a woman with unbound feet wouldn't <u>of</u> [have] found a husband

   easily. Yu-fang's younger sister was luckier. She could have suffer the same fate, but

   by 1917, the practice of foot-binding <u>had</u> [has] been abandoned.

3 • When she was fifteen, Yu-fang became a concubine for a much older man, General

   Xue. She <u>would liked</u> [would had liked] to be a first wife instead of a concubine, but she had no

   choice. General Xue built a large house for Yu-fang, and he stayed with her for one

   week. Then he left her alone for the next six years. Yu-fang can't leave the house.

4• In one generation, life in China changed drastically. Chang's mother had more freedom than women of her grandmother's generation. During the 1950s, her mother studied medicine, but she coulda *could have* studied something else. She married a soldier, but she *could have* coulda chosen another man for a husband.

❯ Take Another Look

Answer the following questions. If you don't know an answer, go back and review the appropriate section.

1• Underline three modals that express possibility. Circle two modals that express advice.

<u>could</u>   have to   <u>may</u>   (should)   <u>might</u>   must   (ought to)

2• Underline the negative form that means "it is not an obligation."

must not   <u>don't have to</u>

3• Underline and correct the errors involving modal or verb forms in the following sentences.

Example: I <u>coulda</u> helped you yesterday.   *could have*

a) You should've went to Calgary.   _____

b) I really <u>gotta</u> find a better job.   *got to*

c) When I was a child, I can ran really fast.   _____

Final Review ❯

Underline and correct fifteen errors involving modal forms.

Example: You should <u>reading</u> Julia's letter.   *read*

Dear Anne,

1• I <u>gotta</u> *got to* tell you about my adventures. As you know, I recently returned from a business trip to England. While I was there, I made some mistakes that I <u>coulda</u> *could have* avoided. Before I left, I should found out about British expressions and customs.

2• For example, soon after I arrived, I met a man on the airport bus. When I mentioned where I was staying, he chuckled and called my hotel a "tip." I can't understand what he meant. I should have <u>ask</u> *asked* him to explain himself. When I arrived at the hotel, I learned that the term means "a big mess."

3• At my hotel, I was given the keys to a tiny room on the fourth floor. It was hard to climb the stairs every day, but I could ~~doing~~ _do_ it. When I looked at the room, I noticed that the wallpaper was peeling and the bathroom was dirty. Clearly, I should ~~of~~ _have_ done more research before making the reservations.

4• The next day, I had to worked at 10 a.m. First, I went into a restaurant for breakfast. I noticed an item on the menu called "Bubble and Squeak." I didn't know what it was, but I ordered it anyway. I must _have_ been crazy because the awful meal consisted of overcooked cabbage and potatoes. After my meal, I asked the waiter to direct me to the ladies' room. The waiter looked suspicious. I should ~~of~~ _have_ said, "Where is the loo?" Then he ~~woulda~~ _would have_ directed me to the appropriate place.

5• In spite of my language blunders, I thoroughly enjoyed my stay. You should ~~to~~ _got to_ go to London, but you ~~gotta~~ find a better hotel than the one I stayed in. Please contact me soon. When ~~you can~~ _can you_ phone me? Where ~~I should~~ _should I_ contact you?

Julia

Wrap Up

Give Advice
With a partner, read the following letters. Give advice and suggestions to each letter writer.

1• My best friend, Jared, got married last year. One night about a month ago, I saw his wife with another man, and they were holding hands. I immediately called Jared and told him about it. Now he is getting a divorce, but he is mad at me! What should I have done?

Adam

2• Last night, I visited some friends. Their daughter, Amy, threw a toy at my son's head. My friends ignored the incident. Then Amy sat on my lap and slapped my face. My friends didn't react and just laughed. I decided to discipline Amy. I scolded her and slapped her hand. She cried, and her parents were furious with me. What should I have done?

Tam

3• Last week, while I was at a club, another guy made a pass at my girlfriend. I hit the guy in the face and knocked him out. Now I have to go to court on assault charges, and my girlfriend is mad at me. Was I wrong? What else should I have done?

_Ed_

Conditional Sentences

In a **conditional sentence**, there is a condition and a result. This type of sentence usually contains two clauses. The main clause depends on the condition set in the *if* clause. There are three conditional forms.

Types of Conditional Sentences

1. Possible Future

Use the "possible future" form when the condition is true or possible.

If + present tense ➡	present or future tense

Condition (*if* clause)	Result
If you **think** about it,	life **is** pretty fantastic.
If you **quit** your job,	you **will have** to find another one.

2. Unlikely Present

Use the "unlikely present" form when the condition is not likely and probably will not happen.

If + past tense ➡	*would* (expresses a condition)
	could (expresses a possibility)

Condition (*if* clause)	Result
If I **won** money in a lottery,	I **would build** a house.
If Eva **knew** how to speak Greek,	she **could take** the job in Athens.

Tip

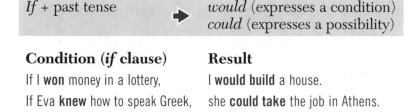

If I Were
In informal English, you occasionally hear *was* in the *if* clause. However, in academic writing, when the condition is unlikely, always use *were* in the *if* clause.

If I **were** rich, I would buy a new car.

If my sister **were** rich, she would spend a lot on clothing.

3. Impossible Past

Use the "impossible past" form when the condition cannot happen because the event is over.

> *If* + past perfect tense ➡ *would have* (+ past participle)
> *could have* (+ past participle)

Condition (*if* clause)	**Result**
If my grandfather **had won** money,	he **would have given** it away.
If you **had told** me about the problem,	I **would have stopped** the project.

EXERCISE 1 ❯ Identify the types of conditional sentences below and write *A* (possible future), *B* (unlikely present), or *C* (impossible past) in the spaces provided.

Example: If he gets the job, he will be really happy. _____A_____

1 • If Eduardo were younger, he would return to school. _____B_____

2 • If you want to learn about sculpting, he will teach it to you. _____A_____

3 • If he had tried harder, perhaps he would have sold more sculptures. _____C_____

4 • Metal sculpting isn't difficult if you learn to weld properly. _____A_____

5 • If he had worn goggles, he would not have injured his eye. _____C_____

6 • Today, if he takes it easy, he can give three classes a week. _____A_____

7 • He would give more classes if his doctor permitted it. _____B_____

8 • Perhaps if he had not sculpted, he would have felt unfulfilled. _____C_____

EXERCISE 2 ❯ Choose the correct form of the verbs below. Decide if the situation is possible or unlikely. Use the possible future or the unlikely present conditional forms.

Example: If you play the scales every day, you (improve) _____will improve_____ a lot.

1 • Adam McClure loves sketching house plans. If he can get a student loan, McClure (try) _____ to complete a university degree in architecture. He would like to build his mother a house one day. "If I (have) _____ a million dollars, I would design and build her a beautiful house," he says.

2 • If Adam didn't need the money, he (study) _____ full time. Unfortunately, he has to work and go to school at the same time. Adam plans to ask his aunt for a job. "If she (help) _____ me, I will be eternally grateful," he says. "If she (help, not) _____ me, I will also understand."

EXERCISE 3 ❯ Complete the following sentences using the impossible past conditional form.

Example: If Welles had had a longer life, maybe he (produce) _would have produced_ another great movie.

1 • Many simple actions can have cataclysmic consequences. Back in 1938, a young actor produced a radio play. Orson Welles' drama about an alien invasion caused panic. If Welles (produce, not) _____ the play, he may never have become famous. On the other hand, those who knew Welles claim that even if *War of the Worlds* had never been produced, Welles (do) _____ something remarkable.

2 • Later in his career, Welles filmed *Citizen Kane,* a thinly-veiled biography of the wealthy newspaper magnate, W. R. Hearst. Hearst was furious. If Hearst (be) _____ able to stop Welles' film, he (do) _____ it. As it was, none of Hearst's newspapers talked about the movie, and it didn't do well at the box office. If Hearst (leave) _____ Welles alone, the movie (make) _____ much more money than it did.

EXERCISE 4 ❯ Write the correct conditional form of the verbs in parentheses.

Example: If the miners (go, not) _had not gone_ on strike, their working conditions would have remained unsafe.

1 • If you do research on the Internet, you (learn) _____ that truck driving is one of the most dangerous professions. William Roach is a long-distance trucker, and he took a truck-driving course in 1992. If he (fail) _____ the course, he would never have found his passion.

2 • Roach loves driving. "On a highway, with nothing but the road in front of me, I feel alive and free. Even if someone offered me a better job, I (remain) _____ a truck driver." Roach claims that the only drawback is the time he spends away from his family. He says, "If I (be) _____ able to, I would bring my wife and son with me."

3 • In 2003, Roach was late for a delivery. To save time, he took an unfamiliar route. While driving, Roach fell asleep, and his truck rolled into a ditch. If he (have) _____ a nap earlier that day, perhaps he (not, have) _____ the accident. If he (stay) _____ on the main highway, perhaps the accident would have involved more vehicles. According to medical professionals, if Roach had stayed awake during the accident, his injuries (be) _____

more severe. Because he was asleep, his body was relaxed and his injuries were

minor.

4 • Roach claims that even if he (know) _____ about the

dangers involved in truck driving, he would still have chosen to become a long-distance

driver. If you could, (you, become) _____

a long-distance driver?

Problems with the Past Conditional

In "impossible past" conditional sentences, the writer expresses the wish that a past
event had worked out differently. It is important to avoid the following errors.

- Do not use *would have* in the *if* clause. Use the past perfect tense instead.

> had asked
> If you ~~would have asked~~ me, I would have travelled with you.

- Do not write *woulda* or *would of* as they are non-standard forms. When
  you use the past forms of *would* and *could*, always include *have* and the
  past participle.

> have
> If you had done your homework, you would ~~of~~ passed the course.

Tip

Avoid Mixing Conditional Forms
If you are discussing a past event, use the third conditional form. Do not mix the second and
third forms.

> had been
> If I ~~were~~ there, I would have done the assignment.

EXERCISE 5 Underline and correct nine errors involving conditional forms.

> *would*
> **Example:** Maybe if I tried harder, I <u>will</u> succeed.

1 • Many people dream of becoming business owners. If you are able to have your own

business, what type of business would you own? My father owns a dog-grooming

business. If I want to, I can join his company. However, I am very allergic to dogs.

Maybe if I weren't allergic, I will consider his offer.

2 • One of the world's most successful companies began in a small village in Sweden. In 1943, seventeen-year-old Ingvar Kamprad did well in his studies, and his father gave him a gift of money. If Kamprad would have bought a car or other material possessions, the money would have disappeared. The young man had other ideas. He decided to create a company called IKEA, and he sold small items through a mail-order catalogue.

3 • In 1947, Kamprad decided to add furniture to his inventory. One day, an employee from IKEA removed the legs from a table so that it would fit into his car trunk. Soon the company created flat packaging designs. If the employee woulda owned a truck, perhaps IKEA would of continued to sell completely assembled furniture. If that had been the case, the company would not of been so successful.

4 • Kamprad's extreme youth helped him in his quest to take chances. Maybe if he woulda been older, he woulda been more conservative. If IKEA would not have changed, perhaps it would have remained a small company.

Making a Wish
Wish about the Present

You make a wish when you want things to be different. When you wish about a present situation, use the past tense.

> I wish I **had** a great singing voice.
> (I can't sing, but I would like to.)

When you wish to change a habit, use *would* or *could*.

> I wish you **would stop** smoking.

With the verb *to be*, always use *were* in formal English.

> He wishes that he **were** stronger.

Wish about the Past

When you wish you could change a past situation, use the past perfect tense.

> Leo wishes that he **had told** the truth to his wife.

Class Exercise

Work with a partner. Read the following sentences and make a wish. If the wish is about a past situation, remember to use the past perfect tense.

SAD BUT TRUE ...	I WISH THAT ...
Example: I have no energy.	*I had some energy.*
1 • Margo never visits me.	_____
2 • My brother is unhappy.	_____
3 • My father doesn't have a job.	_____
4 • I can't afford to buy a car.	_____
5 • Leo didn't visit me yesterday.	_____
6 • I slept badly last night.	_____
7 • I am tired.	_____
8 • It is very cold outside.	_____

EXERCISE 6 Write the correct form of the verbs in parentheses.

Example: I wish I (know) _____*knew*_____ the answer, but I don't.

1 • Carol is always busy. She works full time and she has three children. These days, she wishes that she (have) _____ more time to spend with her kids. She also wishes that her children (help) _____ more with the cleaning.

2 • Carol has a horrible boss. He is very unreasonable, and he asks Carol to put in a lot of unpaid overtime. Carol wishes she (have) _____ a better job. Her co-workers wish that their boss (be) _____ more reasonable.

3 • Carol often wishes that she (stay) _____ in school when she was young. She wishes that she (think) _____ more about her future when she was a teenager.

4 • Carol's ex-husband, Angelo, wishes that they (be) _____ still together. In fact, he wishes that he (leave, not) _____ his wife last year. He wishes that they (try) _____ harder to keep the relationship going.

The Difference Between *Hope* and *Wish*

Use *hope* when you want something to happen, but are not sure that it will (or did) happen.

I hope my brother found his car keys.	(I don't know if he found them.)
I hope Joan's boyfriend is a nice guy.	(I am not sure that he is nice.)
I hope that I pass this course.	(I don't know if I will pass the course.)

Use *wish* when you want to alter the present or the past. People wish for improbable or unlikely things.

I wish that I had more money.	(I wish that I could change my present reality.)
I wish he would stop smoking.	(I wish that a bad habit would change.)
I wish I had never met George.	(I wish that I could change a past event.)

> **Tip**
>
> *Hope* or *Wish*
> To express a desire, use *hope*. Don't use *wish* with the present tense.
>
>   hope
> I ~~wish~~ I finish this project soon. I wish I had more time to work on it.

EXERCISE 7   Fill in the blanks with either *hope* or *wish*.

Example: I _____*hope*_____ the bank is still open.

1 • I am looking for a job. I _____ I can find a job in the social work field. I _____ I had more experience.

2 • Next week, I have my final exams. I _____ I pass the exams. I _____ I had paid more attention in class this semester. I _____ that the exams aren't too difficult. This week, I have to study every night. I _____ I had enrolled in fewer classes.

3 • My cousin is coming to visit tomorrow. I _____ he can amuse himself. I _____ I had more time to spend with him. I _____ he understands that I must study a lot.

EXERCISE 8   Underline and correct eight errors involving conditional forms.

                               were
Example: Many people wish that JFK <u>is</u> still alive.

1 • Many mysteries surround John F. Kennedy's death. I wish that investigators discover what really happened. Luckily, there is good evidence. If Zapruder would not have

taken his home movie, we would never have known about the directions of the bullets.

2• The 1964 Warren Commission made many mistakes. If the investigators would have printed the photos of the assassination in the correct order, they would of known that Kennedy's head moved forward after he was hit by the fatal bullet. Investigators decided that Lee Harvey Oswald acted alone and assassinated the president. Many people wish that the government officials would have examined the evidence more closely.

3• It is difficult for Canadians to own and carry firearms. Maybe if Canadians would have more access to weapons, Canada would be a more violent country. Most Canadians support strict gun control, and if the laws will change, many people will protest against them. I wish that the laws don't change.

> Take Another Look

Answer the following questions. If you don't know an answer, go back and review the appropriate section.

1• In each sentence, write the verb *buy* in the correct tense.

   a) I _____ it if I save enough money.

   b) I _____ it if I had a better job.

   c) I _____ it if I had known what a great deal it was.

2• Underline and correct the error in each sentence.

   a) If I would be younger, I would move to New York.

   b) If the public would have known about Senator Klee's problems, they would have voted against him.

   c) Soon Yi wishes that she have more money.

   d) If Soon Yi were at the rally, she would have helped Senator Klee.

Final Review

Part A
Write the correct form of the verbs in parentheses.

Example: If you (work) ___*could work*___ anywhere, where would you work?

1• Certain jobs disappear because of advances in technology or changing habits. In 1949, Joseph Zahn decided to open a hat-making business in Montreal. He created men's felt hats and sold them in his hat store. If he had chosen another profession, he (be) _____ unhappy. Unfortunately, by the 1950s, men stopped wearing hats and Zahn's business suffered.

2• Nowadays, Zahn has no regrets. If he (can) _____ live his life again, he wouldn't change anything. He often says, "If I (have, not) _____ a business failure, I would have become very arrogant." Today, Zahn's son creates handmade hats for private customers. These days, if you (want) _____ a handmade hat, you will pay a lot for it.

3• In the 1990s, many people thought that if they worked with computers, they (have) _____ a job for life. In 1999, Carmen Morales took a nine-month course in webpage building. When she thinks about the past, she wishes that she (chose) _____ a different course. Today, webpage programs are user-friendly. Nowadays, if you (want) _____ to design your own page, you can easily do it by yourself. Morales believes that if she (take) _____ a programming course, she would have found work more easily. Since September, Morales has been taking some business courses because she wants to be an accountant. If she (have) _____ more time and energy, she would also take courses in computer animation. She wishes that she (feel) _____ more energetic.

Part B
Underline and correct five errors involving conditional forms.

I love gliding down a snow-covered hill. I wish I were a professional snowboarder.

I have won several tournaments, and I have a really good chance of winning the next

one. In fact, if I won my next tournament, I will be eligible to join the provincial snowboarding team. If I practise a lot, I'm sure I would win. Last year, I almost won an important competition in Switzerland. However, the day before the competition, I went for a walk, slipped on some ice, and twisted my ankle. I wish I was more careful that day. If I would have known about the accident, I would have stayed in my hotel room! If I had won that Swiss competition, I would of received a large prize.

Wrap Up

If ...
Work alone or with a partner. Create sentences about the following situations. Write your sentences on a separate sheet of paper. For each sentence, explain why you feel the way you do.

1• If you could have a special talent, what type of talent would you like to have?

2• If your parents had had a billion dollars, how would your childhood have been different?

3• If your girlfriend or boyfriend cheated on you, what would you do?

4• If you had lived one hundred years ago, what type of work would you have done?

5• What person do you wish that you had met before he or she died? If you had met that person, what would you have said? (Examples: Mahatma Gandhi, Kurt Cobain, Tupac Shakur, Marilyn Monroe, Napoleon, Pancho Villa, etc.)

6• What two things do you wish you had done in the past?

Review
of Units 1 to 6

 Class Exercise A
Present and Past Tenses

Part A
Fill in the blanks with the present or past tense.

Example: Why (people, believe) ___*do people believe*___ in ghosts?

1 • There (be) _____ many unusual professions in the world. For example, Dennis Smythe is a ghost-hunter. He (search) _____ for ghosts. According to Smyth, most ghosts (appear, not) _____ at night.

2 • Smythe and his colleagues (think) _____ that most ghost sightings have a simple explanation. For example, in 1992, Smythe (go) _____ to a coal-mining town to (investigate) _____ a ghost. While he (look) _____ in the basement of a small house, he (feel) _____ the earth move.

3 • When the movement stopped, the house's owner said, "(the ghost, make) _____ the house move a few seconds ago?"

4 • As the house started to shake again, Smythe replied, "No. Right now the coal mine (use) _____ dynamite."

Part B
Underline and correct the errors involving tense below. Write *C* beside the sentences that are correct.

occur
Example: When did the event <u>occurred</u>?

5 • Why did someone killed Kennedy?

6 • There was three people in the car with JFK.

7 • The Warren Commission tried to discovered what happened.

8 • Today, why do everybody think there was a conspiracy?

9 • My father don't believe in conspiracy theories.

Class Exercise B
Past and Present Perfect Tenses

Fill in the blanks with the simple past or the present perfect tense. Look for key words to help you.

Example: (you, think, ever) *Have you ever thought* about committing a crime?

1• Adam Davey is just sixteen years old, but he (commit) _____ several crimes since he turned twelve. He (steal) _____ cars at least six times. Last March, the police (arrest) _____ him. Adam (spend) _____ last summer in a youth camp for troubled adolescents. In the summer camp, he (receive) _____ counselling.

2• Frank Schmalleger (write) _____ many books about criminal behaviour. In 2001, he (write) _____ *Criminal Justice Today*. According to Schmalleger, psychologists (develop) _____ at least nine different theories to explain the criminal mind.

3• For example, perhaps Adam (have, never) _____ attention from his parents, so he steals in order to get noticed. Perhaps he (see) _____ too many crime shows in recent years. He (be) _____ in a car accident in 2001, so perhaps he (have) _____ a brain injury during that accident. Also, since Adam turned thirteen, his friends (have) _____ a bad influence on him.

4• According to Adam, since he was very young, he (never, be) _____ _____ able to resist temptation. Last summer, Adam's parents (decide) _____ to stop protecting him. "If he commits more crimes, he will have to pay for the consequences," says Mr. Davey.

Class Exercise C
All Tenses (Present, Past, Future, and Perfect Tenses)

Fill in the blanks with the verbs in their proper tenses. Look for key words to help you.

1• (you, think) _____ that you are too sophisticated to give in to mass hysteria? In 1999, many groups (believe) _____ that the world would soon end. In December 1999, my uncle (buy) _____ four hundred cans of food. When I (see) _____ him last March, my uncle said that he (have, not) _____ any cans left because he (give) _____ them all away. Since March, I (speak, not) _____ with my uncle. Next year, when I (have) _____ some free time, I will visit him.

2 • My brother (believe) _____ that witches are evil. Right now, my brother (watch) _____ a silly movie about witches. He (know, not) _____ the true story of witches. In 1691, in Massachusetts, the witch mania began when eight young girls (have) _____ strange symptoms. In February of that year, while a magistrate (question) _____ a family about a series of crimes, two young girls (accuse) _____ some elderly women of being witches. (the state, kill) _____ over twenty innocent men and women in 1692?

Class Exercise D
Modals

Part A
Change the modals in each sentence to the past form.

Example: I *should visit* my mother.   _____ *should have visited* _____

Today	**Yesterday**
1 • Kate *can't watch* the show.	_____
2 • Kate *should try* to relax.	_____
3 • Kate's daughter *has to perform*.	_____
4 • I *would like* to see the show.	_____
5 • I *should buy* tickets for it.	_____

Part B
Underline and correct the errors involving modals below.

6 • In Greek mythology, Icarus thought he can fly.   _____

7 • Should a man should fly with wings made of feathers and wax?   _____

8 • His father said that Icarus should to stay away from the sun.   _____

9 • Why Icarus would disobey his father?   _____

10 • Wings were found on the ocean surface.   _____
      Icarus must had fallen into the water.

11 • That day, Icarus should have listen to his father.   _____

12 • When I was a child, I wanted to fly like a bird   _____
      and can't accept that humans have no wings.

13 • I jumped off the roof because my brother said   _____
      I could fly, but I broke my leg. I should not of
      listened to him!

14 • Now my brother is a pilot, and he can flying a 747.   _____

15 • I would like to be a pilot, so I gotta take some   _____
      lessons.

Class Exercise E
Conditionals, *Wish*, and *Hope*
Write the correct conditional verb forms in the spaces provided.

1 • According to legend, many ships and planes have disappeared in the Bermuda
Triangle area. The area is in a hurricane corridor. If a ship (get) _____
_____ lost next month, it will probably be due to the weather.

2 • In 1872, the crew disappeared from a ship called the Mary Celeste. Some people think
that aliens took the crew, but if aliens (take) _____
the crew, there would have been proof. If there (be) _____
a storm on that day, the crew could have left the ship in a lifeboat. And if the waves had
been high, the lifeboat (sink) _____. If the Mary Celeste
(have) _____ modern communication devices, then
it (send) _____ out a distress signal.

3 • If I (be) _____ able to travel into the Bermuda
Triangle, I would go there. I wish I (have) _____
more money. If I did, I (go) _____ there tomorrow!
Next week, I am applying for a new job, and I really hope I (get)
_____ the job.

4 • If you (examine) _____ most of the Bermuda
Triangle mysteries, you will discover that there are logical explanations for them. If
you (be) _____ a television producer, would you do
a program on the Bermuda Triangle?

Nouns and Pronouns

Nouns

Using the Singular Form

Each and Every

After *each* and *every*, the noun always takes the singular form.

> <u>Each</u> **person** in this family follows the rules. <u>Every</u> **rule** is important.

Sometimes *every* is followed by a compound subject. Notice that the nouns and verb are singular.

> <u>Every</u> **man** and **woman** needs love.

Non-Count Nouns

Most nouns can be counted. For example, *pen* is a count noun. However, *money* is a non-count noun. Non-count nouns cannot be counted and have no plural form. For example, you can say, "I have a lot of money" or "I have some money," but you can't say, "I have two monies." Always use the singular form of non-count nouns.

Here are some examples of non-count nouns. (A more complete list of non-count nouns appears in the *Open Road Grammar Charts*.)

- **Categories of objects:** clothing, equipment, furniture, homework, housework, jewelry, luggage, machinery, money, music, traffic, work
- **Abstract nouns:** advice, attention, behaviour, effort, evidence, faith, information, knowledge, progress, patience, proof, research, time
- **Environmental phenomena:** air, electricity, dust, energy, pollution, radiation, snow, steam

Nouns with a Plural Form but Singular Meaning

Some nouns always have a plural form but a singular meaning. Use a singular verb with these nouns.

economics	mathematics	news	physics	politics

> **Politics** is a dirty business. The **news** is full of political scandals.

 Tip

Always Use Singular Forms of Adjectives
Adjectives have no plural form.

> simple, plausible
> There must be some ~~simples, plausibles~~ explanations.
> (The adjectives are in the singular form. Only the noun takes the plural form.)

Sometimes nouns act as adjectives.

> I have eight **dollars**.   She has a fifty-**dollar** shirt.
> *Dollar* is a noun, and takes an *s*.   *Dollar* acts as an adjective, and does not take an *s*.

Using the Plural Form

One of the and *Each of the*

Use plural forms of nouns that follow *one of the* and *each of the*.

That is <u>one of the best</u> **movies** I have ever seen! I love <u>each of the</u> **actors**.

Kind, *Sort*, and *Type*

Always use the plural form of *kind*, *sort*, or *type* when they refer to more than one kind, sort, or type. Also write the plural form of the noun that follows *of* unless it is a non-count noun.

There are many **kinds** of <u>people</u> in the world.

The store has several **types** of <u>luggage</u>. (Luggage is a non-count noun)

Special Plural Forms

Some nouns always have a plural form. Use a plural verb with these nouns.

glasses   clothes   pants   savings   scissors

My **pants** are in the wash. My **glasses** are on the table.

Spelling of Plural Nouns

- Add *-es* to nouns ending in *s*, *ch*, *sh*, *x*, or *z*.   boss **>** boss**es**

- For most nouns ending in *f*, change *f* to *ves* in the plural form. Note that *beliefs* is an exception.   knife **>** kni**ves**

- When nouns end in consonant + *y*, change *y* to *ies* in the plural form. When nouns end in vowel + *y*, just add *-s*.   lobby **>** lobb**ies**   boy **>** boy**s**

- Many nouns have irregular plural forms.   person **> people**   child **> children**

- Some nouns that are borrowed from Latin keep the plural form of the original language.   analysis **> analyses**   paparazzo **> paparazzi**   medium **> media**

> **Tip**
>
> ### Nouns Ending in *o*
> Nouns ending in *o* may require either an *-s* or an *-es* ending to form the plural. Use your dictionary if you are not sure how to spell a plural form.
>
> **-es ending:**   potato **>** potato**es**   hero **>** hero**es**   tomato **>** tomato**es**
>
> **-s ending:**   video **>** video**s**   photo **>** photo**s**   logo **>** logo**s**

EXERCISE 1 > Change the italicized words to the plural form if necessary. If you can't use the plural form, write *X* in the space provided. If the word ends in *y*, you may have to change the *y* to *i*.

Example: There are many different recording company_*ies*_ in Canada.

1• Every day_____, companies produce many type_____ of new_____

product_____. One of the most important role_____ of advertisers is to make member_____ of the public notice the products. An interesting example involves the singer Sting. In 1999, the former mathematic_____ and physic_____ teacher had just released an album_____ called *Brand New Day*. The problem was that people didn't have a lot of information_____ about it because radio_____ station_____ were ignoring it. The recording company was going to lose million_____ of dollar_____. It had already used up a five-million_____-dollar_____ budget on the project.

2• One of the song_____ had a music video that included a short clip of Sting driving a Jaguar through a desert. Sting's manager had some advice_____ for his client. He said they should offer Jaguar the use of the video in a promotional_____ campaign_____. Sting agreed, and his only condition was that each television viewer_____ must think the "commercial" was really promoting music_____. Jaguar Corporation went for it and paid television_____ network_____ a lot of money_____ to play the video. Within a two-week_____ period, the song shot up the music_____ chart_____ because a large audience heard Sting's song.

EXERCISE 2 ❯ Underline and correct twelve errors involving plural forms below.

music
Example: The magazines were filled with scandals about <u>musics</u> stars.

1• Ours is a fame-obsessed culture. We constantly read about celebritys in the medias. Magazines and newspapers contain storeys that may or may not be true. Although we cannot necessarily trust the informations in tabloids, we eagerly buy them. Celebrity magazines are a billion-dollars industry.

2• Curiously, most peoples, in spite of their professed lack of interest in the topic, eagerly read news about a singer's six-months-old baby or an actor's divorce. They scan the photoes taken by paparazzis.

3• Perhaps this obsession stems from a deep-seated need in people for heros. When they read about the lifes of the rich and famous, they can live vicariously. They dream that perhaps one day they will have the million-dollars home and the adoring fans.

Using Determiners

Many, Few, and *Fewer*

With count nouns, use *many, a few, very few,* and *fewer*.

> Eric has a **few** <u>problems</u>, although he has **fewer** <u>problems</u> than I do.
> He has **many** <u>debts</u>. He owes money to **many** <u>people</u>.

Much, Little, and *Less*

With non-count nouns, use *much, a little, very little,* and *less*.

> Eric needs a **little** <u>advice</u>. He doesn't have **much** <u>information</u> about bankruptcy laws.
> He has **less** <u>knowledge</u> about bankruptcy laws than I do.

Tip

Using *Much*
Only use *much* in negative and question forms. In affirmative forms, use *a lot* instead of *much*, unless you want to stress an excessive amount of something, such as *too much* or *so much*.

>   a lot of
> Kate has ~~much~~ money. She has **so much** free time these days. She has **too much** jewelry.

EXERCISE 3 › Part A
Fill in the blanks with *much* or *many*.

1 • Historians don't have _____ information about the musical genius Frederic Chopin. They know that he had _____ artistic friends. He visited the novelist George Sand _____ times. When Chopin went to London, he couldn't write _____ music because he spent _____ hours with his _____ acquaintances. He didn't spend _____ time alone.

Part B
Fill in the blanks with *little* or *few*.

2 • One of Canada's previous prime ministers was Mackenzie King. Mr. King had a _____ unusual beliefs. Very _____ people knew about his interest in the occult. Each evening, he spent a _____ hours consulting with ghosts. He hoped to get a _____ advice about how to run the country. During his lifetime, very _____ information became public about Mr. King's obsession. A _____ journalists wrote about King, but very _____ attention was paid to the Prime Minister's reliance on the occult.

Part C
Fill in the blanks with *fewer* or *less*.

3• Some scientists take _____ risks than others. For instance, Stanley
Milgram had _____ faith in humans than some of his colleagues. Other
scientists believed that _____ people would follow an authority figure
than Milgram believed. In my college course, we learned some of the experiment's
subjects spent _____ time in front of the electrical panel than others.

Using *This*, *That*, *These*, and *Those*

This refers to something that is near in time or location. The plural form of *this*
is *these*.

> **This** is a great summer. **These** days I love to relax outdoors. **This** sunhat and **these** sunglasses will
> protect me from the UV rays.

That refers to something that is distant in time or location. The plural form of *that*
is *those*.

> Do you know anything about the 1930s? At **that** time, there was a depression. **Those** were difficult
> years. **That** man with the white hat was born in 1930.

EXERCISE 4 > **Part A**

Underline and correct four errors involving *this, that, these,* or *those* in the
paragraph below.

> *These*
> **Example:** <u>This</u> shoes that I'm wearing are too tight.

1• Do you see this green house across the street? Last year, a man lived there, and he
asked me to keep an eye on his house while he was away. At this time, I was not
very busy, so I agreed. A few days later, he asked if I would also water his plants.
Then he asked if I would feed his cat. That weren't difficult chores to do, so I
agreed. My neighbour had used a successful sales method called the "Foot in the
Door" technique. After I had agreed to a small request, I was more likely to agree
to a second, larger request. This days, I have a new neighbour named Veronica.

Part B

Underline the correct answers in parentheses below.
> **Example:** I've been feeling quite lonely (<u>these</u> / those) days.

2• In the early 1900s, (persons / people / peoples) didn't buy many luxuries. In (this /
that / these / those) days, it was difficult to mass-market products. At (this / that /
these / those) time, marketing was done with print ads.

3. Now, (this / that / these / those) days, it is much easier to mass-market products because companies can use the Internet and other forms of media. For example, I bought (that / this) bracelet that I'm wearing on eBay. Look at (this / those / these) earrings that I'm wearing. I also bought them online.

Pronouns

Pronouns replace nouns and noun phrases. A complete list of pronouns appears in the *Open Road Grammar Charts*.

Subject and Object Pronouns

The subject does the action, and the object is affected by the action. Sentences may have more than one subject or object.

She	**them**	**it**
The professor talked to the students about her latest experiment.		
subject	object	object

When a pronoun is paired with another noun, the correct pronoun isn't always obvious. A simple way to determine the correct pronoun is to say the sentence with just one pronoun.

The professor asked Martin and (**I or me**) to present our topic.

Possible choices: The professor asked **I**. / The professor asked **me**.

Correct answer: The professor asked Martin and **me** to present our topic.

Pronouns in Comparisons

When a pronoun follows a comparison that uses *than* or *as*, ensure that you use the correct pronoun. To verify that your pronoun is correct, complete the thought.

I like psychology better than (**he or him**).

Complete the thought: I like psychology better than **he** (likes psychology).

Possessive Adjectives

Don't confuse the following possessive pronouns with similar sounding words.

Its / It's
Its is a possessive adjective.
It's is the contraction of *it is*.

The company unveiled its newest ad.
It's a very effective campaign.

Their / They're / There
Their is a possessive adjective.
They're is the contraction of *they are*.
There indicates that something exists.

Their house is on the edge of a cliff.
They're going to move.
There are many unexplained mysteries.

Your / You're
Your is a possessive adjective.
You're is the contraction of *you are*.

Your painting is beautiful.
You're a great friend.

EXERCISE 5 ❭ Underline the appropriate words in parentheses.

Example: My friend and (<u>I</u> / me) discussed an ethical issue related to families.

1• Jake Rostrum has low self-esteem. He doesn't like (him / himself) very much. (There / Their / They) are many reasons for his problem. (Her / His) father didn't give (her / him / himself) very much attention. His parents are very rich, and they bought (theirselves / themselves / themself) a huge house. They left the child-rearing responsibilities up to (there / their / theirs) nannies and servants.

2• Psychologists have long understood that bonding in the first six months of birth is highly important. In Jake's case, (he / him) and his sister didn't have consistent attention during their early years. The nannies constantly changed because Mrs. Rostrum didn't want the nannies to have a better relationship with the children than (she / her) or her husband.

3• Some psychologists believe that children should develop a strong bond with a parental figure. If the bond is broken, (its / it's) detrimental to the child's development. I hope you have a great relationship with (your / you're) children.

Pronoun Agreement

A pronoun must agree with its **antecedent**, which is the word that the pronoun refers to.

> antecedent
> The <u>Milgram experiment</u> had **its** debut in 1964.

Collective Nouns

Collective nouns such as *army*, *family*, or *association* refer to a group that acts as a unit. Therefore, any pronoun that refers to a collective noun is singular. (A list of collective nouns appears on page **4**.)

> <u>The government</u> will not revise **its** policies.

And / Or

When two or more nouns are joined by *and*, use a plural pronoun to refer to them.

> <u>Milgram</u> and <u>Zimbardo</u> published **their** results.

When the nouns are joined by *or* or *nor*, the pronoun agrees with the noun that is nearest to it.

> Does Milgram or <u>Zimbardo</u> have regrets about **his** experiment?
> Neither the men nor the <u>women</u> removed **their** glasses.

One of the / Each of the

In sentences containing the expressions *one of the* or *each of the,* the subject is the indefinite pronoun *one* or *each.* You must use a singular pronoun to refer to the subject.

One of the women spoke with **her** lawyer.

Indefinite Pronouns

When the antecedent is a singular indefinite pronoun such as *everybody, something,* or *nobody,* use a singular pronoun to refer to it.

At the men's club, nobody had a chance to voice **his** objection to the new rule.

If the gender of the subject is unknown, or if the subject is both genders, use the male and female pronoun. If the sentence appears awkward, simply change the subject to the plural form.

Incorrect: Everybody must submit **their** answers to the professor.

Solution: Everybody must submit **his or her** answer to the professor.

Better solution: The students must submit **their** answers to the professor.

EXERCISE 6 〉 Write appropriate pronouns or possessive adjectives in the spaces provided.

Example: He conducted the experiment in _____*his*_____ laboratory.

1• Solomon Asch was a social scientist. One of his most well-known experiments had _____ debut in 1951. In a small room, he conducted _____ classic study about conformity. He gathered a group, and _____ consisted of about ten participants. The people believed that _____ were in an experiment to test _____ visual judgment. Each person was led into a room filled with other people. What the participants didn't realize was that everybody else in the room had _____ role to play. In fact, all the others were actors except for the subject. Everyone was shown a line, and then _____ had to state which line was similar to the first line. The correct answer, B, would be obvious to the average person if _____ looked carefully.

2• Everyone working for Asch knew that _____ must give the wrong answer. Asch wanted to know if the unsuspecting subject would give the same incorrect answer as the others in the group. In the first test, the male participant listened to the others and then made _____ answer match that of the others in the room. Neither the first nor the second male participant answered correctly even though _____ clearly knew what the correct answer was. In fact, over one third of the participants answered the question incorrectly because they wanted to conform with the group. Those who disagreed with the others in the group expressed extreme discomfort, and _____ fidgeted and appeared nervous.

Avoid Vague Pronouns

When you use pronouns, the antecedent (the person or object that the pronoun refers to) should be clear to the reader. Avoid using confusing pronouns like *it* and *they* that have no clear antecedent.

Vague:	<u>They</u> say that most people are conformists. (Who are they?)
Clearer:	**Psychologists** say that most people are conformists.

Vague:	<u>It</u> said in a magazine that some ads manipulate children. (Who or what is it?)
Clearer:	**A magazine journalist** said some ads manipulate children.

In an essay that contains a repeated pronoun, such as *he* or *they*, make sure that the antecedents are clear.

Many teens try to be rebellious. Maybe they are unhappy and their actions worry their parents.
The parents   *the teens*
<u>They</u> surely want them to be happy and healthy. Sometimes discussions aren't enough for <u>them</u>.
  their parents'
They lose <u>their</u> trust and then they don't know what to do.

Tip

Pronoun Shifts
When you write a paragraph or essay, make sure that your pronouns are consistent. Don't shift pronouns unless you are adding a supporting anecdote and the shift is logical.

Everyone needs to feel loved and respected. When people know that they are important to somebody
    them
else, it helps ~~you~~ to make the correct decisions. For example, my parents always made us feel wanted

and respected.

EXERCISE 7 Underline and correct twelve errors involving pronoun usage in the paragraphs below.

          their
Example: Our guests forgot to bring <u>there</u> luggage.

1• When you travel, there are certain precautions that you should take. They say that

if anyone wants you to carry items across a border, you should tell them that you

can't do it. Its also useful to carry emergency money in a safe place. Finally, we can't

be too careful. If you feel uncomfortable around a stranger, you should trust your

instincts. When your faced with a crisis, you will know how to react.

2• Last summer, my brother and me learned about travel safety the hard way. While

we were waiting in a train station, we left our bags on the floor. Two young women approached us and started talking to my brother and I. They wanted us to look at there map. Neither the tall woman nor the short woman had their suitcase with them, and one of the women seemed nervous. Suddenly, out of the corner of my eye, I saw a quick movement. A young man had grabbed my suitcase! He ran away, and we couldn't catch him because he ran faster than my brother and me. The two girls we had been with also disappeared quickly. My brother and me should have trusted our instincts, and one of us should have watched the bags.

❯ Take Another Look

Answer the following questions. If you don't know an answer, go back and review the appropriate section.

1 • Underline six non-count nouns in the list below. Remember, non-count nouns don't have a plural form.

advice	animal	assignment	children	dollar	equipment
homework	information	music	person	research	suitcase

2 • Underline and correct the errors in the sentences below. Then write a rule about each error.

    a) He made a two-millions-dollar investment.   _____

    Rule: _____

    b) In 1992, I had a good year. This year, I earned a lot of money.   _____

    Rule: _____

    c) I needed more informations about the product.   _____

    Rule: _____

    d) There were less customers at the bank today than there were yesterday.   _____

    Rule: _____

3 • Underline the correct pronouns in parentheses below.

    a) You should lock (you're / your) car doors unless (it's / its) a very old vehicle.

    b) Neither Jake nor his brother ate (his / their) supper.

    c) Please don't try to sell that product to Tim and (I / me).

    d) Everyone puts useless items in (their / his or her) kitchen drawer.

    e) You earn more money than Bruno or (I / me).

Final Review

→

Part A
Underline the appropriate words in parentheses below.

1• A common sales method is called the "lowball technique" and it is used by (much / many) car dealers, politicians, and real-estate agents. Those who avoid the technique have (less / fewer) sales than those who use it. A customer is offered a product for (less / fewer) money than it seems to be worth. After the customer accepts the deal, the cost of the commitment increases and the deal has (less / fewer) advantages than it appeared to have at first.

2• For example, my husband and (I / me) bought our first new car last August. We had just moved out of the city, and neither the bus nor the subway had (their / its / it's) route near us. We really needed a car, and (these / those) cars in the showroom were very appealing. Of course, in all new car dealerships, each of the cars costs more than

(its / they're / he's / it's) really worth. When we entered the car showroom, we had very (few / little) (information / informations) about cars. We should have asked friends for some (advice / advices) before shopping for a new car.

3• On (this / that) day, one of the (salesman / salesmen) acted very persuasively. He told my husband and (I / me) that he would reduce the price quite dramatically. We could have a five-(thousand / thousands)-(dollar / dollars) discount. He had our attention, and we agreed to the deal. As we were signing the contract, the dealer announced that there would be a few extra charges. The floor mats, hubcaps, sound system, and a few other (piece / pieces) of (equipment / equipments) would cost extra. We would also have to pay a "transportation" fee of almost two (thousand / thousands) dollars. Finally, there would be a three-(week / weeks) delay before we could get our car. Still, we had agreed to the initial deal and didn't back out when the extra demands were made.

Part B
Underline and correct five errors involving nouns, pronouns, or determiners.

4• Most persons are easily manipulated. Consumers receive very few information about medias and marketing techniques. This days, everybody should take their time to learn about consumer psychology.

Adjectives and Adverbs

Adjectives

Adjectives describe nouns (people, places, or things) and pronouns (words that replace nouns). They add information explaining how many, what kind, or which one.

COMPARATIVE AND SUPERLATIVE FORMS OF ADJECTIVES		COMPARATIVE	SUPERLATIVE
A. Add -er or -est to one-syllable adjectives.	short	shorter than	the shortest
When adjectives end in a consonant-vowel-consonant, double the last letter.	hot	hotter than	the hottest
B. In two-syllable adjectives ending in consonant + y, change the y to i and add -er or -est.	easy	easier than	the easiest
C. Add more or most to adjectives of two or more syllables and to compound adjectives.	modern well-behaved	more modern than more well-behaved than	the most modern the most well-behaved
D. Irregular adjectives	good bad much/many little far	better than worse than more than less than farther/further*	the best the worst the most the least the farthest/ the furthest

* Farther indicates a physical distance. Further means "additional." For example: I need further information before I can make a decision.

EXERCISE 1 Complete the sentences with the appropriate comparative or superlative forms. Remember to add *than* or *the* when necessary.

Example: In the 1970s, men's hair was (long) ___*longer than*___ it is today.

1• The women in the 1920s were (wild) _____ in previous generations. Their dresses were (short) _____ their mother's dresses.

2• Louise Brooks was (famous) _____ "flapper" of the 1920s. She was (famous) _____ Clara Bow.

Louise was also (good looking) _____ Clara.
However, Clara was (funny) _____ Louise.

3• The U.S. government prohibited the sale of alcohol in the 1920s. Buying alcohol was (difficult) _____ it is today.

4• In the 1920s, people listened to jazz music. Some people believe that jazz is (good) _____ type of music that has ever been invented. My brother thinks that punk music is (good) _____ jazz. However, my brother has (bad) _____ taste in the world. My father listens to (little) _____ amount of music possible because he hates music.

> **Tip**
>
> **Comparative Form**
> Usually *the* is used in superlative rather than comparative forms. However, there are some two-part comparatives that require the use of *the*. In these expressions, the second part is the result of the first part.
>
>   action   result
>   **The more** you exercise, **the better** you will feel.

EXERCISE 2 ❯ Underline and correct eight errors involving comparative forms.

                             funniest
Example: That was the <u>most funny</u> movie I've ever seen.

1• Some people think that the most they give their children, the happiest their children will become. However, money seldom makes people feel best. In fact, when sociologists examined the children of the most wealthiest Canadians, they discovered that the children's lives weren't better than the lives of their peers. In fact, in many ways, the lives of the wealthy offspring were much worst. Children of the rich had more higher drug abuse rates, and in surveys they consistently said that they felt less fulfilled than their peers. One child of a billionaire had the less amount of self-esteem of all the children who were studied. On the other hand, the study proved that the most a child is loved, the better he or she will feel, regardless of the family's income level.

Adverbs

An adverb is any word (or group of words) that adds information to a verb, adjective, or another adverb. Most adverbs end in -*ly*, but there are some exceptions.

COMPARATIVE AND SUPERLATIVE FORMS OF ADVERBS		
	COMPARATIVE FORM	**SUPERLATIVE FORM**
Regular -*ly* Adverbs nicely quietly beautifully	more nicely than more quietly than more beautifully than	the most nicely the most quietly the most beautifully
Irregular Adverbs (no -*ly*) close late fast low hard often high soon	faster than harder than more often than sooner than	the fastest the hardest the most often the soonest
Other Irregular Adverbs well badly much	better than worse than more than	the best the worst the most

Tip

Spelling of Adverbs
When a word ends in *l*, form the adverb by adding -*ly*.

careful + *ly*
The team of historians worked **carefully**.

When a two-syllable word ends in *y*, form the adverb by changing the *y* to *i* and adding -*ly*.

happy + *ly*
They worked together **happily**.

EXERCISE 3 ❯ Decide if the italicized words are adverbs or adjectives. Add -*ly* when necessary. If no -*ly* is required, put an X in the space.

Example: The musician wrote music very slow ___*ly*___ .

1 • Beethoven was an extremely *serious*_____ musician. He played the piano *beautiful*_____ . He *often*_____ composed his music at night. He could write a sonata *quick*_____ .

2 • When he was thirty years old, his hearing loss was *undeniable*_____. He became *serious*_____ depressed. He also became *extreme*_____ creative.

3 • In this "middle" period, his work was very *successful*_____. He *successful*_____ completed many symphonies. He became *firm*_____ established as the greatest composer of his era.

Placement of Frequency Adverbs

Frequency adverbs, words such as *always*, *often*, *sometimes*, *usually*, or *ever*, indicate how often someone performs an action or how frequently an event occurs.

- Place frequency adverbs before regular present and past tense verbs.

    John Lennon **sometimes** <u>travelled</u> to Japan.

- Place frequency adverbs after the verb *to be*.

    Yoko <u>was</u> **often** very busy.

- Place frequency adverbs after auxiliary verbs.

    She <u>had</u> **never** been in the public eye before.

Tip

Real vs. *Really*
Real is an adjective that means "genuine" or "not fake."

   He bought his girlfriend a **real** diamond.

Really is an adverb that means *in reality* or *actually*. *Really* also expresses the degree to which something is true. Note that you can substitute *really* with *very*, but you can't substitute *real* with *very*. Also, never put *very* before a verb.

                                    really
   They worked **really** hard on the song. I ~~very~~ like David's voice.

Ensure that you always modify verbs using an adverb.

                    really loudly
   John Lennon sang ~~real loud~~ during his performance of "Give Peace a Chance."

EXERCISE 4 ❭ Underline and correct ten errors involving adjective and adverb forms and word order.

                              often contain
   Example: Newspapers and magazines <u>contain often</u> articles about the love affairs of the rich and famous.

1 • One of the greatest love stories of the twentieth century was the romance between John Lennon and Yoko Ono. In 1967, John met Yoko in a gallery where she exhibited sometimes her artwork. John climbed up a ladder and carefuly examined a tiny painting. On the painting was the word *yes*, and John very liked the fact that the message was positive. His relationship with Yoko Ono progressed real quick.

2 • When John married Yoko, the press followed often them. When they walked in New York's Central Park, they usually were chased by photographers. The couple also had a real difficult time because Beatles fans didn't accept Yoko. In 1973, the couple broke up, but John eventualy realized that he wanted to be in New York with the love of his life. They lived really happy until John's unfortunate death in 1980.

Equality: *As ... As / The Same As*

Both *as ... as* and *the same as* express equality.

> Sharon is **as nice as** Doug.   Her last name is **the same as** mine.

Sometimes one object isn't *as good as* another.

> High heels are **not as comfortable as** running shoes.

EXERCISE 5 > Write the correct form of the words in parentheses. You may need to change an adjective to an adverb. You will need to supply the following words: *than* or *as ... as*.

1 • When he was young, my father was a good athlete, but he started smoking when he was twenty-seven. As a young man, his lungs were much (healthy) _____ they are today. These days, he can't run (quick) _____ he used to.

2 • In past decades, smokers didn't have (many restrictions) _____ _____ they have today. They smoked (free) _____ _____ they do these days at work, in restaurants, and in all other public places. On the other hand, the workplace environment wasn't (pleasant) _____ it is today. The health of non-smokers was (bad) _____ it is today. These days, workplace conditions are much (good) _____ they were in the past.

Good and *Well* / *Bad* and *Badly*

Good is an adjective, and *well* is an adverb.

> Adjective   They had a very **good** relationship.
> Adverb   They communicated really **well**.

Exception: Use *well* to describe a person's health.

> She is not <u>well</u>. She has the flu.

Bad is an adjective, and *badly* is an adverb.

> Adjective   Yoko was not a **bad** singer.
> Adverb   However, some critics reacted **badly** to her work.

EXERCISE 6 > Underline the correct adjectives or adverbs in parentheses below.

> **Example:** Some people can play music really (good / <u>well</u>).

1 • The singer known as Pink was born Alecia Moore in 1979. During her teen years, she (regular / regularly) performed at Club Fever. On stage, she danced quite (bad / badly). However, she sang really (good / well). One night, a representative

from MCA Records spotted her and asked her to audition for the band Basic Instinct. Pink tried to work with the band, but it ended (bad / badly). Their communication wasn't very (good / well). In 1998, Pink decided to become a solo artist. Her first album, *Can't Take Me Home*, was released in 2000. The album sold really (good / well). It was a double-platinum hit.

❯ Take Another Look

> Answer the following questions. If you don't know an answer, go back and review the appropriate section.
>
> Underline and correct the errors in the sentences below.
>
> **1•** If you complain, it will make things <u>worst</u> than before. _____
>
> **2•** Carol has as much money <u>than</u> I do. _____
>
> **3•** Bill is a <u>more better</u> businessman than Donald. _____
>
> **4•** The harder you work, the <u>worst</u> you will feel. _____
>
> **5•** Alex does the <u>less</u> amount of work of anyone that I know. _____
>
> **6•** Pink sings <u>real</u> <u>good</u>. _____

Final Review ❯

Part A

Write the correct form of the words in parentheses. You may need to change an adjective to an adverb. You will need to supply the following words: *the, than,* or *as ... as.*

Example: Picasso's work is (valuable) <u>*more valuable than*</u> the work of other artists.

1• Pablo Picasso is considered one of (lucky) _____ artists of the twentieth century. He could sell paintings (easy) _____ artists of his generation. In fact, he dominated western art. Some historians estimate that by 1920, over a hundred million people had heard about his work. Even Michelangelo's audience was (small) _____ Picasso's audience.

Self-portrait (1907) by Pablo Picasso; oil on canvas; Narodni Gallery, Prague

2• When Picasso painted, his goal was to elicit (strong) _____ feeling possible in others. He worked (fast) _____ most other artists, and the effects he achieved were extremely powerful. Picasso believed that he wasn't (talented) _____ Goya, but he also knew that he wasn't (conventional) _____ his idol.

3 • Near the end of his life, Picasso worked much (obsessive) _____ he did during his youth. In fact, his seventies and eighties were (productive) _____ years of his life. However, some critics believe that his later work was much (bad) _____ his earlier work. In fact, some say that during his last ten years, he produced (bad) _____ art of his entire career.

4 • Still, even when he was ninety, Picasso's paintings sold (quick) _____ the work of any other living artist.

>>> "The Two Saltimbanques" (1901) by Pablo Picasso; oil on canvas; Pushkin Museum, Moscow

Part B
Underline and correct the errors involving adjective or adverb forms in the sentences below. Write *C* beside the sentences that are correct.

Example: His early work wasn't his <u>more</u> interesting work.   *most*

5 • Picasso knew that he was real good at stirring up strong sentiments in people.   _____

6 • The more Picasso painted, the better he felt.   _____

7 • When Picasso turned ninety, the Louvre honoured him by inviting his most greatest friends to a celebration of his life and work.   _____

8 • When Picasso arrived at the celebration, he walked really slow, but his eyes were bright, and it was perhaps the happiest day of his life.   _____

9 • Picasso believed that his love life was the less interesting thing about him.   _____

10 • His children have said that his parenting skills weren't as good than his artistic ones.   _____

11 • His many ex-wives and mistresses have also complained that he was least attentive to them than he should have been.   _____

12 • In spite of his personal problems, Picasso has become a cultural icon, and he is one of the most famous people of the twentieth century.   _____

Word Form

The Passive Voice

Look carefully at the following two sentences. Notice the differences between the active and the passive voice.

Kurt wrote that story in 1961.   This is active because the subject (*Kurt*) did the action.

The story **was written** in 1961.   This is passive because the subject (*the story*) was affected by the action. The subject didn't do the action.

The passive voice is formed by the verb *to be* + the past participle. It is preferable to use the active voice except when emphasizing the action and not the doer of the action. The passive voice should be used sparingly.

Active and Passive Forms

	ACTIVE (The subject does the action.)			PASSIVE (The subject receives the action.) *to be* + past participle		
VERB TENSES						
Simple present		make			<u>are</u> made	
Present progressive		are making			<u>are being</u> made	
Simple past	They	made	shoes.	Shoes	<u>were</u> made	by them.
Present perfect		have made			<u>have been</u> made	
Future		will make			<u>will be</u> made	
MODALS						
can		can make			**can be made.**	
could		could make			**could be made.**	
should	He	should make	shoes.	Shoes	**should be made.**	
would		would make			**would be made.**	
must		must make			**must be made.**	
TO BE						
Use the past participle after *to be*. Children need **to be seen** but not **heard**.						

EXERCISE 1 Decide if the underlined verbs below are active or passive. Write *A* for "active" or *P* for "passive" above the verbs.

                                               P   A

Example: Many ordinary citizens <u>have been recruited</u> as spies even though the work <u>is</u> dangerous.

1 • During times of war, armies <u>have used</u> both scouts and spies. Army scouts <u>can wear</u> their full uniform. They <u>are sent</u> ahead of advancing forces. Spies, on the other hand, <u>wear</u> disguises and <u>try</u> to blend in with the regular population.

2 • Spying <u>is</u> much more dangerous than scouting because captured scouts <u>are treated</u> as prisoners of war. A captured spy, on the other hand, <u>may be executed</u> immediately. In spite of the obvious dangers, many people <u>are attracted</u> to the field of espionage because they <u>love</u> excitement and danger.

EXERCISE 2 **Part A**
Complete the following sentences by changing the verbs in italics to the passive form. Don't alter the verb tense. Note that you don't always have to include the *by* … phrase.

    Example: The supervisor *spies* on the workers.
                 The workers *are spied on (by the supervisor).*

1 • Sometimes employers *place* spy cameras in their factories.

Sometimes spy cameras _____

2 • Last year, Mr. Roy *installed* three surveillance cameras.

Last year, three surveillance cameras _____

3 • The video cameras *filmed* some sleeping workers.

Some sleeping workers _____

4 • As a result, the boss *has fired* three technicians.

As a result, three technicians _____

Part B
Complete the following sentences by changing the verbs in italics to the active voice. Don't alter the verb tense.

    Example: The workers *are spied on* by the bosses.
                 The bosses *spy on the workers.*

5 • For months, Reginald's privacy *has been violated* by the cameras.

For months, the cameras _____

6 • Last week, a complaint *was made* to the police by Reginald.

Last week, Reginald _____

7. The case *will be investigated* by the union.

The union _____

8. Complaints about privacy *are often ignored* by companies.

Companies often _____

More on Using the Past Participle

Use the past participle:

- of verbs that follow *to be*.

    I want to be **discovered**. She needs to be **seen** to be **believed**.

- of verbs that follow *have*, *has*, or *had* in perfect tenses.

    I have **seen** many films. My sister has never **owned** a television.

Use the base form:

- of most verbs that follow the word *to*.

    She wanted to **study** with me. I told her to **wait** until tomorrow.

- of verbs that follow modals (*can, could, should, would, must, may, might*).

    He can **study** with us. You should **ask** him about it.

- of verbs that follow the auxiliaries *do*, *does*, or *did* in questions and negative forms.

    Did he **study** with you yesterday?

    He generally doesn't **study** with me.

> **Tip**
>
> Verb Form
> **Sometimes *be* is suggested but not written.**
> Sometimes the passive voice can be written with just the final verb. Look at the following
> sentence. It has the passive form, so the past participle must be used.
>
>   **Example:** Many activities **done** in the 1920s are still common today.
>
>   ^
>   Missing words: *that were*
>
> **Never write *to don't*.**
> When you use a negative infinitive, just put *not* before the infinitive.
>
>   **not to do**
>   I asked you ~~to don't do~~ that.

EXERCISE 3 > Underline and correct twelve errors involving verb form below.

               enjoyed
Example: I have <u>enjoy</u> some great spy novels.

1. British authors have create some of the best spy novels. John Le Carré was really

name David Cornwell, and he was born in Dorset, England, in 1931. In 2000, in a documentary with the British Broadcasting Corporation, Le Carré admitted that he was recruit by the British spy agency, the M15, in 1959. He spied for many years, and when he studied at Oxford, he was asked to spied on fellow students. Officials asked him to don't tell anyone about his job.

2. Le Carré has an interesting past. He was raise by his father, Ronnie Cornwell, who was a charismatic con artist. When the senior Cornwell was arrested, he had already swindle millions of British pounds. Le Carré didn't meet his own mother until he was twenty-one. After one visit, he asked her to don't visit him again. Le Carré didn't want his name to be link to his infamous father. Many of Le Carré's novels were influence by his childhood experiences.

3. Although many spy novelists are British, the first complete spy novel, wrote by American author James Fenimore Cooper, was publish in 1852. *The Spy* was about soldiers during the American Revolution.

Choosing *-ing* or *-ed*

Some adjectives look like verbs because they end in *-ing* or *-ed*.

- When the adjective ends in *-ed*, it describes the person's or animal's expression or feeling.

   The **interested** audience listened to the presentation.

- When the adjective ends in *-ing*, it describes the quality or state of the person or thing.

   The **interesting** speaker described his experiences in Beijing.

EXERCISE 4 Underline the appropriate word in parentheses.

1. My neighbour greatly dislikes the (annoyed / annoying) pigeons that gather on his balcony. He isn't (suppose / supposed / supposing) to hurt the birds, but he often throws rocks at them. He doesn't realize that the pigeon is a (fascinating / fascinated) bird with an (interesting / interested) history.

2. Richard Platt, in his book *Spy*, describes the pigeon's (excited / exciting) role during past wars. According to Platt, homing pigeons were (use / using / used) by military personnel to pass (interested / interesting) secret messages. The (appreciated / appreciating) birds had great endurance and could fly over enemy territories. (<u>Overworked</u> / Overworking) enemy forces would stare at the sky, never realizing that the (passed / <u>passing</u>) birds were working for their opponents.

Recognizing Gerunds and Infinitives

Sometimes a main verb is followed by another verb. The second verb can be a gerund or an infinitive. A **gerund** is a verb with an *-ing* ending. An **infinitive** consists of *to* and the base form of the verb.

Verb + gerund   We <u>finished</u> **reading** *Wild Swans*.

Verb + infinitive   I <u>want</u> **to write** about it.

Some verbs in English are always followed by a gerund. Do not confuse gerunds with progressive verb forms. Compare a progressive verb and a gerund.

Progressive verb   Julie is studying now.   Julie is in the process of doing something.

Gerund   Julie <u>finished</u> **studying**.   *Studying* is a gerund that follows *finish*.

Some Common Verbs Followed by Gerunds

acknowledge	deny	loathe	recollect
adore	detest	mention	recommend
appreciate	discuss	mind	regret
avoid	dislike	miss	resent
can't help	enjoy	postpone	resist
complete	finish	practise	risk
consider	involve	quit	tolerate
delay	keep	recall	

Some Common Verbs Followed by Infinitives

afford	decide	manage	refuse
agree	demand	mean	seem
appear	deserve	need	swear
arrange	expect	offer	threaten
ask	fail	plan	volunteer
claim	hesitate	prepare	want
compete	hope	pretend	wish
consent	learn	promise	would like

Some Common Verbs Followed by Gerunds or Infinitives

Some common verbs can be followed by gerunds or infinitives. Both forms have the same meaning.

begin	continue	like	love	start

Elaine <u>likes</u> **to read**. Elaine <u>likes</u> **reading**.

(Both sentences have the same meaning.)

EXERCISE 5 > Underline the correct words in parentheses.

1 • People plan (to betray / betraying) their country for many reasons. According to Christopher Andrew, co-author of *The Sword and the Shield*, the word MICE explains why a person might agree (to become / becoming) a traitor. MICE means "Money, Ideology, Compromise, and Ego."

2 • According to Andrew, some people enjoy (to spend / spending) money so much that they will betray their country for cash. They can't resist (to have / having) extra luxuries. Others hope (to have / having) some excitement in their lives. They don't mind (to do / doing) dangerous acts.

3 • Sometimes people decide (to believe / believing) in another ideology. They promise (to support / supporting) a country with different political views. Others can't avoid (to be / being) manipulated. In a court case, Max B. mentioned (to become / becoming) a spy because someone blackmailed him.

4 • When Andrew finished (to write / writing) his book, he was surprised at the response. People really like (to read / reading) about spies.

Stop, Remember, and Used To

Some verbs can be followed by either a gerund or an infinitive, but there is a difference in meaning depending on the form you use.

TERM	FORM	EXAMPLE	MEANING
stop	+ infinitive	He stopped <u>to buy</u> gas every Sunday.	To stop an activity (driving) in order to do something
	+ gerund	I stopped <u>smoking</u> five years ago.	To permanently stop doing something
remember	+ infinitive	Please remember <u>to lock</u> the door.	To remember to perform a task
	+ gerund	I remember <u>meeting</u> him in 1985.	To have a memory about a past event
used to	+ infinitive	Jane used <u>to smoke</u>.	To express a past habit
	+ gerund	Jane is used <u>to living</u> alone.	To be accustomed to something

EXERCISE 6 > Underline the correct words in parentheses.

1 • Do you remember (using / to use) a cellphone camera for the first time? When I first got my phone, I remember (to take / taking) pictures of my ear when

I accidentally hit the camera button. My grandfather doesn't have a cellphone and (isn't used to speaking / didn't use to speak) on them. He forgets which buttons to push. The next time I visit him, I must remember (to show / showing) him how to use one because I would like (buying / to buy) him a cellphone.

2• My grandfather (used to be / is used to being) uncomfortable around computers. He was a technophobe. Now he uses computers every day, and he (used to work / is used to working) on a computer. He knows how to send e-mails, although he wishes that salespeople would stop (to send / sending) him junk mail.

3• Today, on my way home from work, I stopped (visiting / to visit) my grandfather. Recently, he stopped (smoking / to smoke), and I am so relieved. He coughs a lot. Probably he should have stopped (smoking / to smoke) years ago.

Prepositions plus Gerunds

Many sentences have the structure *verb + preposition + object*. If the object is another verb, the second verb is a gerund.

I dream <u>about travelling</u> to Greece.

Some Common Verbs Followed by Prepositions plus Gerunds

accuse of	(be) excited about	(be) good at	prohibit from
apologize for	feel like	insist on	succeed in
discourage <u>him</u> from*	(be) fond of	(be) interested in	think about
dream of	forbid <u>him</u> from*	look forward to	(be) tired of
(be) enthusiastic about	forgive <u>me</u> for*	prevent <u>him</u> from*	warn <u>him</u> about*

* Certain verbs can have a noun or a pronoun before the preposition.

EXERCISE 7 ⟩ Fill in the blanks with the correct preposition and gerund.

Example: Jeremy was enthusiastic (sell) ___*about selling*___ cellphones.

1• When cellphone cameras first came out, I looked forward (own) _____ one. I felt (buy) _____ an expensive model. I soon learned that many people have used cellphones inappropriately.

2• Many people insist (take) _____ pictures in public places. In 2003, many health clubs forbade clients (use) _____ the phones. Some customers were accused (take) _____ photos in the locker rooms. One voyeur refused to apologize (disrespect) _____ people's privacy.

3• Additionally, government workers have complained about the possible misuse of cellphone cameras in public places. In 2004, an astute member of the public succeeded (record) _____ one government employee's rage. However, she had to apologize (invade) _____ the employee's privacy. If you are interested (own) _____ a cellphone camera, ask people for permission before you take their photos.

❯ Take Another Look

Answer the following questions. If you don't know an answer, go back and review the appropriate section.

1• Write the verb *sell* in the correct passive form on the blanks below.
Example: Every day, many books _are sold._

   a) Last week, a new article _____ by the journalist.

   b) Next year, a new book _____ by Simmons Press.

   c) Since 1990, over five hundred books _____ by Simmons Press.

2• Write the correct gerunds or infinitives in the spaces provided.
Sara Redmond enjoys (fly) _____. She wants (be) _____ a pilot. She hopes (get) _____ her pilot's license next March. Her mother said, "Stop (take) _____ those lessons." However, Sara will finish (study) _____ next month. She will become a pilot, and her mother can't prevent her from (do) _____ it.

3• Underline and correct the error in each sentence.

   a) Last year, Raoul developed a severe cough, so he stopped to smoke. Now he is a non-smoker.

   b) Sophie tries to don't eat a lot of meat.

   c) Raoul hates exercise, and he refuses walking in the woods.

   d) Sophie avoids to be in the house while Raoul practises playing folk songs.

Final Review ❯

Part A
Underline the correct words in parentheses.

Example: I would like (<u>to know</u> / knowing) more about Navajo code talkers.

1• Although I usually avoid (to do / doing) extra work, I am interested (to learn / learning / in learning) to speak Navajo. It is a complex language with no alphabet or written form. During World War II, Navajo natives agreed (making / at making / to make) an important contribution to the Allied war effort.

2 • During the war, Japanese and German technicians succeeded (tapping / to tap / in tapping) Allied communication lines. Japanese code breakers enjoyed (solving / to solve) Allied code language, and they were good (to understand / understanding / at understanding) it. When they finished (learning / to learn / at learning) a code, the code became useless for the Allies. The Japanese and German code breakers managed (figuring / to figure) out every code that the Allies came up with.

3 • In 1942, hundreds of Navajo volunteers offered (to help / helping) the Allied forces. At that time, only about thirty non-natives had managed (learning / to learn) Navajo. The Navajos were enthusiastic (to relaying / relaying / about relaying) coded messages using Navajo words. Thus, fighter planes (were calling / called / were called) "hummingbirds" and submarines were "iron fish." The Navajos were prohibited (discussing / to discuss / from discussing) their work with others.

4 • Some former Japanese code breakers remember (to spend / spending) hours working on the codes, but they never learned (to solve / solving) the Navajo code.

Part B
Make the following sentences passive. Don't alter the verb tense.

    Example: The code breakers didn't understand the code.
             The code _wasn't understood (by the code breakers)._

5 • The volunteer repeated the code word.
    The code word _____

6 • They couldn't break the code.
    The code _____

7 • Many stores sell the book.
    The book _____

8 • Directors will make more movies about the war.
    More movies _____

9 • Since the 1970s, journalists have contacted former code breakers.
    Since the 1970s, former code breakers _____

Combining Sentences and Common Sentence Errors

Sentence Combining

To make your writing more interesting, you can combine sentences in a variety of ways. Review the following sentence types.

A **simple sentence** has one independent clause (complete idea).

The fraud victims went to court.

A **compound sentence** contains two or more independent clauses (complete ideas) joined by a coordinating conjunction. You know a sentence is compound when you can cover the coordinating conjunction (*and, but, or,* or *so*) and still have two complete sentences.

The fraud victims went to court, **and** they asked for compensation.

A **complex sentence** contains at least one independent clause and one dependent clause (incomplete idea). A dependent clause "depends" on another clause in order to be complete. A dependent clause usually begins with a subordinator such as *after, although, because, unless,* or *when.*

dependent clause   independent clause
Because they had lost their life savings, the fraud victims went to court.

You can also combine compound and complex sentences. The next example is a **compound complex sentence**.

complex
Although Karina is tiny, she is strong, and she is a very effective police officer.
compound

Connecting Ideas in Compound Sentences

To create compound sentences, join two ideas with a coordinator. The most common coordinators are:

and   but   or   so

EXERCISE 1 ▷ Fill in each blanks with the appropriate coordinating conjunctions. Note that some sentences may have more than one answer.

Example: In 1969, the FBI introduced criminal profiling as an investigative strategy, ___*and*___ it has been quite successful.

1•Kim Rossmo is a renowned geographic profiler, _____ he is also an excellent detective. In the early 1990s, Detective Rossmo could work in Canada,

_____ he could take a job in the United States. The Vancouver Police Department didn't try to keep Rossmo, _____ he moved south.

2• Rossmo examines the movements of criminals, _____ he searches for specific patterns. According to Rossmo, criminals attack places they know, _____ they generally don't work in their own neighbourhoods.

3• Rossmo developed a fascinating mathematical formula, _____ many police departments were skeptical about his ideas. Basically, he inputs the addresses of suspects into a computer, _____ he also inputs details about the crime scenes. His program can handle a twenty-square-kilometre area, _____ it can find a "hot" area. Suspects may live directly in the centre of the hot area, _____ they may live within a few blocks.

Connecting Ideas in Complex Sentences

Using Common Subordinators

When you add a **subordinating conjunction** to a clause, you make the clause dependent. "Subordinate" means secondary, so subordinating conjunctions are words that introduce secondary ideas.

The police arrived **because** the alarm was ringing.

Meanings of Subordinating Conjunctions

Subordinating conjunctions create a relationship between the clauses in a sentence.

SUBORDINATING CONJUNCTION	INDICATES	EXAMPLE
as, because, since	**a reason or a cause**	He paid a lot <u>because</u> he wanted a good alarm system.
after, before, since, until, when, whenever, while	**a time**	<u>After</u> he drove home, he parked on the street.
as long as, even if, if, unless	**a condition**	The alarm won't ring <u>unless</u> someone touches the car.
although, even though, though	**a contrast**	<u>Although</u> the alarm began to wail, nobody looked outside.
where, wherever	**a location**	<u>Wherever</u> you go, you hear annoying car alarms.

EXERCISE 2 ❯ Add missing subordinating conjunctions to the paragraphs. Use each of the following subordinating conjunctions once only.

   although   because   unless   whenever   after   until   ~~when~~

1• _____ _When_ _____ a new television program about crime scene investigations is announced, many people watch it. Lawyers and prosecutors get annoyed

_____ members of the jury expect to see sophisticated crime solving techniques. It is very expensive and difficult to get DNA analyses _____ the case is very important.

2 • In the late 1990s, _____ several sexual assaults had occurred in an Ontario town, Kim Rossmo and his associates created a profile map. _____ someone seemed like a possible suspect, the person's name would be placed in Rossmo's computer program. _____ one particular offender's name was low on a list of 316 suspects, it rose to number six on the list after the profiling. The suspect didn't admit his guilt _____ other evidence tied him to the crime scenes, He was eventually tried and convicted for the crimes.

Using Relative Clauses

Some complex sentences contain relative clauses. A relative clause begins with a **relative pronoun**. Review the following terms.

COMMON RELATIVE PRONOUNS	
Use **who** or **whom** to give information about people. (*Whom* is used in formal English to represent the object of the verb.)	• The man <u>who</u> committed the crime looks very ordinary. • The man <u>who(m)</u> you met is a police officer.
Use **that** to give information about people or things.	• The case <u>that</u> the detective investigated was baffling.
Use **which** to give additional (non-essential) information about things.	• The movie, <u>which</u> has become a classic, stars Colin Farrell.
Use **where** to give information about a place.	• The city <u>where</u> I was born is beautiful.
Use **when** to give information about a time.	• She will always remember the moment <u>when</u> the police solved the case.
Use **whose** to show possession. *Whose* can replace *his, her, its,* or *their.*	I saw a woman. **Her** eyes were blue. ▼ I saw a woman <u>whose</u> eyes were blue.

Tip

Using *That* or *Which*
Both *that* and *which* refer to things, but *which* refers to non-essential ideas. Also, *which* can imply that you are referring to the complete subject and not just a part of it. Compare the next two sentences.

The shirts **that** had stains provided DNA evidence.
(This sentence suggests that some shirts had no stains.)

The shirts, **which** had stains, provided DNA evidence.
(This sentence suggests that all of the shirts had stains.)

EXERCISE 3 ❭ Fill in the blanks with *who, whom, that, which, where, when,* or *whose*. Note that in some cases, more than one answer is possible.

Example: Last night, I read a story ____*that*____ was true.

1 • Last week, my friend had an experience _____ was upsetting.

2 • She described the moment _____ she met her brother for the first time.

3 • Maya went to a coffee shop _____ she ordered some breakfast.

4 • A man _____ she had never met sat at her table.

5 • The man told her a story _____ was about his father.

6 • The man, _____ name is William, told Maya that he was her long-lost brother.

7 • Their father, _____ seemed to be in a happy marriage, had had an affair.

8 • Maya, _____ had always been an only child, discovered that she had a half brother.

9 • A psychologist wrote a book _____ focuses on sibling reunions.

10 • Her book, _____ became a bestseller, says that siblings share a special connection.

Tip

Commonly Confused Words

Whose or Who's
Who's is the contracted form of *who is.*   **Who's** at the door?
Whose indicates possession and replaces *his, her, its,* or *their.*   **Whose** car is that?

Who or Whom
Who is the subject of the clause.   The detective **who** specializes in arson wrote a book.
Whom is the object of the clause.   The detective **whom** we met was helpful.

Than, Then, or That
Than is used to compare two things.   She is older **than** I am.
Then means "at a particular time."   He graduated, and **then** he found a job.
That introduces a clause.   The book **that** I read is very good.

EXERCISE 4 ❭ Underline and correct twelve errors involving *who, whom, which, than, then, that,* and *whose*. Look for incorrect or misspelled words.

than
Example: In the past, prisons were less comfortable <u>then</u> they are today.

1 • Charles Dickens was a man which lived in London in the 1800s. It was a time when

laws were very harsh. Dickens' father, who's name I now forget, was a businessman

who owed money to several bankers. The people to who he was indebted were not very forgiving.

2• When Charles Dickens was twelve years old, his father was taken to Marshalsea Debtor's Prison. It was a moment who changed the life of the boy. The prison, wich was a filthy, crowded place, had no separate sections for males and females. Before his father left, Charles asked him, "Whose going to take care of us?" His father just lowered his head sadly.

3• Young Charles had no choice but to leave school. Than, for the next six months, he worked in a factory than made shoes. The money who he earned helped him support his siblings. The experience, who was very difficult, also provided Dickens with material that he would later incorporate into his novels.

4• Charles Dickens, a talented writer who's work is well known, wrote *David Copperfield* and *Great Expectations*. The books, who became very popular, are about working-class youths, and both books mention Debtor's Prison.

Making Embedded Questions

When you combine a question with another sentence, remove the auxiliary or place it after the subject.

Question	**Embedded Question**
Why do people commit crimes?	He asked <u>why people commit crimes.</u>
How should we proceed?	I wonder <u>how we should proceed.</u>

Use *if* or *whether* if there is no question word.

Was he convicted?	Do you know <u>**if** he was convicted?</u>

Tip

Use the Correct Word Order
When you edit your writing, ensure that you have formed your embedded questions properly.

she thought
Dr. Alvarez wonders why ~~do~~ people commit crimes. I asked her what ~~did she think~~ about the issue.

Combining Sentences and Common Sentence Errors •• UNIT 10

EXERCISE 5 ❭ Complete the embedded questions below.

Example: What does he want? I wonder _____ *what he wants.*

1• How old is the suspect? Do you know _____

2• Why was she arrested? I wonder _____

3• Does she have an alibi? Can you tell me _____

4• Where did the crime occur? I don't know _____

5• Should we watch the trial? I wonder _____

6• What will the jury decide? We discussed _____

EXERCISE 6 ❭ Underline and correct six errors involving embedded questions.

Example: The writer explains how ̲c̲a̲n̲ ̲p̲e̲o̲p̲l̲e̲ become criminals.
people can

1• Many experts wonder why is the crime rate so high. Parents may ask how are role models a factor. They question how do negative models influence youths. Some blame icons in youth culture. For example, a newspaper recently linked the hateful words of gangster rappers to youth crime.

2• However, it is unclear how can people only point the finger at singers or other celebrities from youth culture. In fact, they should really ask why are so many "pillars" of society deviant. Corporate executives have stolen from shareholders, and prominent religious figures have promoted intolerance and hatred. A reporter from Halifax asks why have so many people in highly regarded positions of authority abused their power. Psychologists, sociologists, and criminologists are trying to find answers.

Common Sentence Errors

Identifying Fragments and Run-Ons

A sentence must have a subject and a verb, and it must express a complete idea. A **fragment** is an incomplete sentence. In the following examples, the fragments are underlined.

No verb	̲F̲i̲r̲s̲t̲,̲ ̲m̲e̲m̲b̲e̲r̲s̲ ̲o̲f̲ ̲t̲h̲e̲ ̲m̲e̲d̲i̲a̲. They were at the trial.
No subject	The lawyer was very calm. ̲Q̲u̲e̲s̲t̲i̲o̲n̲i̲n̲g̲ ̲t̲h̲e̲ ̲s̲u̲s̲p̲e̲c̲t̲.̲
No main clause	The defendant was convicted. ̲A̲l̲t̲h̲o̲u̲g̲h̲ ̲h̲e̲ ̲w̲a̲s̲ ̲i̲n̲n̲o̲c̲e̲n̲t̲.̲

Tip

Adding Examples
When you add an example to prove a point, be particularly careful that your sentence is complete. The next fragments were taken from student essays.

> For example, when they made the prisoners clean toilets in "The Stanford Prison Experiment."
> Like Milgram's experiment when people obeyed an authoritarian figure.

A **run-on** occurs when two or more complete sentences are incorrectly connected. Note that you can't join two complete sentences with a comma.

> The case went to court, the evidence was compelling.

EXERCISE 7 ⟩ Write *F* beside the fragments and *RO* beside the run-ons below. Write *C* beside the sentences that are correct.

Example: Circumstantial evidence is often discounted.   *C*

Although it may be reliable.   *F*

1 • Circumstantial evidence is often very reliable.   _____

2 • Blood evidence, for example.   _____

3 • It may match with the DNA of the victim, it may not.   _____

4 • Pieces of clothing, hair fibres, and other types of evidence.   _____

5 • Such evidence is usually very good.   _____

6 • Somebody altered the evidence, it is no longer useful.   _____

7 • A credit card may place a criminal at the crime scene.   _____

8 • Although the suspect may have an alibi.   _____

How to Correct Fragments

To correct a fragment, join it to another sentence or add the missing subject or verb.

Fragment	**Correction**
First, members of the media.	First, members of the media **were at the trial**.
Questioning the suspect.	**The lawyer was very calm while** questioning the suspect.
Although he was innocent.	**The defendant was convicted**, although he was innocent.

How to Correct Run-Ons

A run-on sentence can be corrected in the following ways.

> Run-On: The case went to court, the evidence was compelling.

Make two sentences:	The case went to court. **T**he evidence was compelling.
Add a subordinator:	**When** the case went to court, the evidence was compelling.
Add a coordinator:	The case went to court, **and** the evidence was compelling.
Add a semicolon:	The case went to court; the evidence was compelling.

EXERCISE 8 ⟩ Underline and correct eight errors involving fragments and run-ons in the paragraphs below. Use a variety of correction methods.

> Example: The case was over, the defendant was innocent.
>
> (semicolon inserted: over; the)

1• In the past, lab technicians looked at evidence through a microscope, they might examine a strand of hair. A comparison of hair samples. It could deliver a conviction.

2• In recent years, scientists have developed more sophisticated techniques. Such as computer imaging. Dr. Edward Blake is a leading authority on DNA evidence, he often testifies at trials. According to Dr. Blake, microscopic hair analysis is subjective. Although it has secured convictions in many cases.

3• In 1993, Billy Gregory's hair matched a hair found at a crime scene. The strands of hair had exactly the same colour and width, they were genetically different. In 1993, Gregory was convicted of the crime and sentenced to life in prison. In 2000, a DNA test cleared him, he was able to go home.

4• Today, conventional hair comparison evidence is no longer allowed in most courtrooms, it may become an obsolete science.

Faulty Parallel Structure

Pairs or groups of items in a sentence should have a balanced grammatical structure. Faulty parallel structure occurs when equivalent ideas are presented with different grammatical structures.

Not parallel:	The detectives worked slowly and were careful.
Parallel adverbs:	The detectives worked <u>slowly</u> and <u>carefully</u>.
Not parallel:	They were people who were trained, who were professional, and having high standards.
Parallel clauses:	They were people <u>who were trained</u>, <u>who were professional</u>, and <u>who had high standards.</u>

When you identify faulty parallel structures, look at the repeated grammatical units and then rewrite the unit that isn't parallel.

EXERCISE 9 ⟩ Underline and correct the errors involving parallel structure. Write *C* beside the sentences that are correct.

> Example: I enjoy reading and <u>to learn</u> about psychology. _____*learning*_____

1• In the 1930s, some doctors, psychologists, and people who do research tried to identify the causes of aggressive behaviour.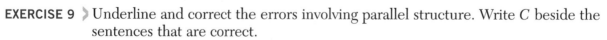

UNIT 10 ·· Combining Sentences and Common Sentence Errors   © Pearson Longman – Reproduction prohibited

2 • The scientists knew that their work was exciting and a challenge.   _____

3 • In 1939, experimenters removed the temporal lobe from some monkeys that were friendly, active, and who had good health.   _____

4 • After the surgery, the monkeys showed absolutely no fear of snakes or humans.   _____

5 • The doctors determined that the amygdala plays a role that is essential and has significance in fear responses.   _____

6 • The scientists hoped to learn more about how humans anticipate and dealing with fear.   _____

7 • In 1966, a man named Charles Whitman acted strangely and with violence.   _____

8 • Before his death in a shootout with police, Whitman wrote a note and was asking doctors to examine the state of his brain.   _____

9 • In fact, a later examination revealed the presence of a tumour next to his amygdala.   _____

10 • Scientists believe that damage to the frontal lobe can contribute to behaviour that is controlling, sadistic, and causes people to abuse others.   _____

> **Tip**
>
> **Be Careful with Long Sentences**
> If your sentence is too long, it may be difficult for the reader to understand. Also, you may accidentally write run-on sentences. If you have any doubts, break up a longer sentence into shorter ones.
>
> **Long and complicated:** In his book *Criminal Justice Today*, Frank Schmalleger describes a practice done by the ancient Hebrews who sometimes punished a tribe by sending a sacrificial goat into the wilderness and the goat, which was supposed to symbolically contain the tribe's sins, became the source of the modern word *scapegoat*.
>
> **Better:** In his book *Criminal Justice Today*, Frank Schmalleger describes a practice done by the ancient Hebrews. They sometimes punished a tribe by sending a sacrificial goat into the wilderness. The goat, which was supposed to symbolically contain the tribe's sins, became the source of the modern word *scapegoat*.

Edit the following long sentence by breaking it into smaller sentences. You can remove some words. Make sure that you punctuate each sentence correctly.

1 • In the eighteenth century England sent convicts to the American colonies and to Australia and the program which was known as transportation had two purposes and the goals were to rid Britain of undesirable criminals but also to provide a captive force of workers who could help build roads and housing for the people who were developing the colonies so although many criminals had to go on long journeys and would never see their families again they also had a much better life than they would have had if they had remained in Great Britain's damp and overcrowded prisons and therefore some may have been grateful for the chance to build a new life in a different country.

❯ Take Another Look

Answer the following questions. If you don't know an answer, go back and review the appropriate section.

Correct the errors in the sentences below. Then write a rule explaining each error.

1 • First, the strangest experiment.

Rule: _____

2 • A scientist conducted a test who was very successful.

Rule: _____

3 • The test was about altruistic behaviour, it was fascinating.

Rule: _____

4 • I wondered why did they make the test.

Rule: _____

5 • The researcher was helpful, friendly, and acted with generosity.

Rule: _____

Final Review

Part A

Circle the letter of the correct answer. Note that *X* means "nothing."

1 • In the 1980s, crime rates were high in Canada and the United States ... they have fallen since then.

    a) ,   **b)** ;   **c)** :   **d)** X

2• Our city made a study … was about crime rates.

    a) that   **b)** who   **c)** wich   **d)** whom

3• The former mayor of New York, … term lasted from 1994 to 2001, thinks that community policing helped reduce crime.

    a) who   **b)** which   **c)** who's   **d)** whose

4• Community policing, … was an idea that Giuliani supported, began in the late 1990s.

    a) that   **b)** who   **c)** which   **d)** whom

5• Officers patrol small areas, they get to know the local people … they stop people from committing minor crimes.

    a) , and   **b)** ; but   **c)** : although   **d)** ,

Part B

Underline and correct the errors in the sentences below.

    Example: I read an article <u>who</u> discusses gun control.   _that_

6• Americans can easily buy guns, Canadians must get special permits.   _____

7• In 2003, only 538 murders in Canada.   _____

8• Some politicians suggest than the economy has contributed to lower crime rates.   _____

9• There are fewer crimes. Because the unemployment rate is low.   _____

10• When people have jobs, they are less likely to be aggressive, anti-social, and act with violence.   _____

Part C

Make the following questions embedded. Remember to change the position of the verb, if necessary.

    Example: Where are we? Do you know _____ _where we are ?_ _____

11• What is the problem? Do you know _____

12• Why did the crime rate drop? I wonder _____

13• Where are the criminals? Can you tell me _____

14• How have the police reacted? I don't know _____

15• When should we discuss it? I wonder _____

Punctuation and Capitalization

Punctuation

Apostrophe (')

Use an apostrophe

- to join a subject and verb together.
  to join an auxiliary with *not*.
  (Exception: *will + not = won't*)

We**'re** tired.
He should**n't** stay.

- to indicate possession.
  Add **'s** to singular nouns even when
  the noun ends in *s*.
  Add **'** after the *s* on plural nouns.
  Add **'s** to irregular plural nouns.

Helen**'s** house and Jess**'s** car
the students**'** lockers
the women**'s** department

> **Tip**
>
> **Possessive Form of Compound Nouns**
> When two people have joint ownership, add the apostrophe to the second name. When two
> people have separate ownership, add apostrophes to both names.
>
> | Joint ownership | Marian and **Jake's** gallery is successful. |
> | Separate ownership | **Marian's** and **Jake's** studios are in different buildings. |

EXERCISE 1 Write the possessive forms of the following phrases.

Example: the sister of the doctor

the doctor's sister

1 • the brush of the artist

the artist's brush

2 • the brushes of the artists

the artists' brushes

3 • the pictures of Sandra

Sandra's pictures

4 • the room of the child

the child's room

5 • the rooms of the children

the children's room

6 • the photo of Ross and Anna

Ross' and Anna's photo

7 • the photo of Ross and the
photo of Anna

Ross' photo and Anna's photo

Common Apostrophe Errors

Don't use apostrophes before the final *s* of a verb or a plural noun.

       wants   galleries

   Mr. Garcia ~~want's~~ to open several ~~gallery's~~.

In negative contractions, remember that the apostrophe replaces the missing *o*.

    doesn't

He ~~does'nt~~ understand the problem.

EXERCISE 2 ❯ Underline and correct fifteen errors involving apostrophes. Note that you may need to add, remove, or move apostrophes.

                 artist's

Example: What is an artists motivation to create?

1 • In 1982, Dr. Teresa Amabile made an interesting study in creativity. For Amabile's study, she divided schoolgirl's into two groups. Both groups rooms were filled with collage material, including coloured paper, paste, and construction paper. The doctor chose collage-making because it doesn't require drawing skills.

2 • Both groups were invited to an "art party" in separate rooms. The first group's goal was to create art in order to win a prize, such as a nice toy. The doctor offered toys to the best three artists. Thus, the children's motivation to create was to win the exciting prize. The girls in the second group didn't have to compete for a prize. They were simply told that three name's would be randomly drawn for prizes.

3 • The doctor's hypothesis was that people's creativity would lessen if they created in order to win a reward. Amabile asked local artists to judge the collages when the children weren't in the room. The judges scores for the first group were consistently lower than those for the second group. Thus, the doctor's hypothesis was correct. A reward, such as money or a prize, isn't helpful to the creative process. When people create art for arts sake, they tend to be more imaginative.

Comma (,)

Use a comma

- to separate three or more words in a series. (Place a comma before the final *and*.)

    The doctor was small, wiry, and smart.

- after an introductory word, phrase, or idea.

    After the experiment, he left the room.
    When I find a better job, I will move.

- between the parts of a compound sentence, which is a sentence that contains at least two complete ideas. (Place the comma before *and*.)

    Childhood has three stages, and each stage is equally important.

- around interrupting phrases that give additional information about the subject.

    Alan, an electrician, earns a good salary.

- in quotations, after an introductory phrase.

    Picasso said, "Find your passion."

> **Tip**
>
> **Common Comma Errors**
> If a sentence begins with a dependent clause (a clause beginning with a subordinator such as *although* or *because*), place a comma after it. However, if the dependent clause appears in the middle of the sentence, no comma is necessary. Notice the difference in the next two sentences.
>
> Comma   <u>Because rents are so high</u>, some young adults live with their parents.
>
> No comma   Some adults live with their parents because rents are so high.
>
> Don't separate the subject and verb with a comma.
>
>   The researcher/was surprised with the results of the experiment.

EXERCISE 3 Add the missing commas or remove the unnecessary commas in the sentences below. Write *C* beside the sentences that are correct.

Example: Erik Erikson, a child development expert, wrote about his identity crises.

1 • In *Childhood and Society*, Erik Erikson explained his views about

    the stages of life. _____

2 • Erikson said, "There are eight life stages." _____

3 • Each stage, in his opinion, is characterized by a developmental crisis. _____

4 • In the infancy stage, babies must learn, to trust others. _____

5 • When babies are neglected, they may end up mistrusting the world. _C_

6 • Babies become extremely anxious, when they are not held and caressed. _____

7 • Adolescents may have an identity crisis, because they face physical

    and emotional turmoil. _____

8 • In Erikson's view, each crisis must be solved before a person

    develops in the next life stage. _____

Which, That, and Who

Review the comma rules in clauses beginning with *which*, *that*, and *who*.

Which

Always use commas to set off clauses beginning with *which*.

> The brain, **which is a complex organ**, develops rapidly.

That

Don't use commas to set off clauses beginning with *that*.

> The house **that I grew up in** was demolished last year.

Who

When a clause begins with *who*, you may or may not need commas. If the clause contains non-essential information, put commas around it. If the clause is essential to the meaning of the sentence, it does not require commas.

Essential	Many people **who have brain injuries** undergo subtle personality changes. (The underlined clause is essential to understand the meaning of the sentence.)
Not essential	Dr. Jay Geidd, **who lives in Maryland**, made an important discovery. (The underlined clause contains extra information, but if you removed the clause, the sentence would still have a clear meaning.)

EXERCISE 4 › Edit the following paragraphs by adding ten missing commas.

Example: The neurologist, who I have never met, made an exciting discovery.

1 • Twenty years ago, scientists thought that the brain stopped changing at an early age. After children reached twelve years of age, their brains would stop growing. In 1997, a team of doctors who specialized in brain research made an exciting discovery. Neuroscientist Dr. Jay Giedd, who works at the National Institute of Mental Health, realized that brain cells have a growth spurt just before puberty. Scientists made another discovery. Myelin, which connects brain cells, increases during adolescence. The last region to receive myelin is the frontal lobe.

2 • The frontal lobe, which is responsible for rational decision making, stops the individual from making impulsive choices. For example, imagine that you are driving your car. When another car cuts you off, the primitive part of your brain wants to hurt the other driver. The frontal lobe helps you think about alternatives. Thus, you may simply accept that all drivers make mistakes.

3 • According to specialists, teens may have trouble curbing their impulses. They may react quickly, violently, or irrationally. When the frontal lobe has fully developed, people generally become less impulsive.

Semicolon (;)

Use a semicolon to join two complete but related ideas.

> I think computers are a necessity. My dad refuses to use one.
>
> ⌄
>
> I think computers are a necessity; my dad refuses to use one.

A complete sentence can begin with the following transitional expressions. If you join such a sentence with another, put a semicolon before the transitional expression and a comma after it.

furthermore   however   in fact   moreover   nevertheless   therefore

> I showed my dad how to use a computer. Nevertheless, he won't use one.
>
> ⌄
>
> I showed my dad how to use a computer; nevertheless, he won't use one.

Colon (:)

Use a colon

- after a complete sentence that introduces a quotation.

    Cartier Bresson stated his view: "Photographers are dealing with things that are continually vanishing."

- to introduce a series or a list after a complete sentence.

    A child goes through several stages: connection, release, and reconnection.

- after the expression *the following*.

    Please do the following: read, review, and respond.

- to separate the hour and minutes in expressions of time.

    The exhibit will open at 12:15.

Hyphen (-)

Use a hyphen

- with some compound nouns. (Note that *compound* means "more than one part.") The next nouns always require a hyphen.

    mother-in-law   show-off   sister-in-law

- when you write the complete words for compound numbers between 21 and 99.

    twenty-five   ninety-two   seventy-seven

- after some prefixes such as *ex-, mid-,* or *self-*.

    ex-husband   mid-December   self-assured

- when you use a compound adjective before a noun. The compound adjective must express a single thought.

    one-way street   thirty-year-old woman   well-known actor

There is no hyphen if the compound adjective isn't before the noun.

> The street is one way.   She is thirty years old.   The actor was well known.

If the adjectives before a noun function independently, don't add a hyphen.

> No hyphen: Lange was a motivated, creative woman.
> (The two adjectives function separately.)

Non-Hyphenated Compound Adjectives
Some compound adjectives never take a hyphen, even when they appear before a noun.

World Wide Web   high school senior   real estate agent

EXERCISE 5 > Add the missing punctuation marks to the following sentences. The number of missing punctuation marks is indicated in brackets.

Example: [1] When Florence and Cleo Thompson were living in Merced Falls, the 1929 stock market crash devastated the economy.

1 • [1] Cleo Thompson was thirty-two years old when he died unexpectedly.

2 • [4] Florence Thompson, a single mother, stooped over in fields to pick the following items: strawberries, peas corn, and asparagus.

3 • [2] One day, Florence was in a tent by the highway waiting for her son to return, it was a day that would make her famous.

4 • [3] Dorothea Lange, a photographer, was travelling home at 3:30 p.m. when she saw a sign for a migrant camp.

5 • [1] Lange described what happened that day: "I approached the hungry and desperate mother, as if drawn by a magnet."

6 • [2] Sitting in her dust-covered canvas tent, Florence Thompson was holding her baby.

7 • [1] The next day, Lange published the photos in a San Francisco newspaper.

8 • [1] Concerned citizens sent the following: tins of food, tents, and building supplies.

9 • [2] However, Florence Thompson wasn't there to see the outpouring of generosity, because her brother-in-law had brought her to his home.

10 • [1] The compassionate photographs of Dorothea Lange, which have appeared in thousands of books, have influenced modern documentary photography.

>>> Migrant Mother

Quotation Marks (" ")

When you insert quotations in your essays, it is important to punctuate them properly. Use **quotation marks** to set off the exact words of a speaker or writer. If the quotation is a complete sentence, there are some standard ways that it should be punctuated.

- Capitalize the first word of the quotation.
- Place quotation marks around the complete quotation.
- Place the end punctuation inside the closing quotation marks.

Oscar Wilde declared, "All art is useless."

Attach the name of the speaker or writer to the quotation in some way. Review the next rules.

1 • Introductory Phrase

When the quotation is introduced by a phrase, place a comma after the introductory phrase.

Pablo Picasso said, "Art is a lie that makes us realize the truth."

2 • Interrupting Phrase

When the quotation is interrupted, place the comma after the first part of the quotation, and place another comma after the interrupting phrase.

"In the end," says dancer Martha Graham, "it all comes down to breathing."

3 • End Phrase

When you place a phrase at the end of a quotation, end the quotation with a comma instead of a period.

"Great art picks up where nature ends," said Marc Chagall.

If your quotation ends with other punctuation, put it inside the quotation mark.

"Who is the greatest painter?" the student asked.

"That question cannot be answered!" the curator replied.

4 • Introductory Sentence

When you introduce a quotation with a complete sentence, place a colon (:) after the introductory sentence.

George Balanchine explains his philosophy: "Dance is music made visible."

5 • Inside Quotations

If one quotation is inside another quotation, then use single quotation marks (' ') around the inside quotation.

Bernice was forced to act: "She turned to Charlie Paulson and plunged. 'Do you think I ought to bob my hair?'"

6 • Integrated Quotation

If the quotation isn't a complete sentence, and you simply integrate it into your sentence, don't capitalize the first word of the quotation.

Dorothy Nixon calls herself a "terrible mother."

Page or Paragraph Numbers

If you are quoting a source and have a page reference, put the page or paragraph number in parentheses. Place the final period after the parentheses.

In his essay, Levi says, "We were interchangeable" **(4).**

Ellipses [. . .]

Use ellipsis marks [. . .] to show that you have omitted unnecessary information from a quotation. When you type the three periods, leave a space before and after each period, and put square brackets around the ellipses.

Seligman wrote, "The path is very clear. [. . .] We must work together."

Using Ellipses [. . .]

Only delete non-essential information from a quotation. When you delete essential information, the quotation is no longer understandable. For example, a student wrote the following lines. Do you see the problem?

Paul wants Diana to become a jealous wife: "She will not like [. . .] afraid of the pretty girls you may meet."

Because so much of the quotation has been deleted, it is incomprehensible.

EXERCISE 6 In each sentence, the quotation is set in bold. Add capital letters, quotation marks, commas, or colons to the quotations as necessary.

Example: Professor Wayne Johnson asks , "**W**here are the great female artists?"

1 • Art student Alex Beale says, "**The lack of great female artists throughout history is puzzling**"

2 • Professor Aline Melnor states , "**One must consider the conditions for producing art**"

3 • "**Art schools didn't accept women,**" she points out.

4 • "**Until a hundred years ago, the only alternative to family life for women was the convent,**" proclaimed writer and feminist Germaine Greer.

5 • "**The painter Suzanne Valadon,**" says historian Maria Sage, "**went from being an artist's model to being an artist.**"

>>> Untitled painting (1912) by Suzanne Valadon

6 • Germaine Greer's book shows the connection between female and male artists **,** **The painter Rosa Bonheur learned about art from her father, who was also an artist . (117)** **"**

7 • Angel Parerra told her mother **" I know that I shouldn't have drawn on the walls, but you always say   Express yourself .** **"**

8 • In her book, Louise Otto-Peters expresses a strong opinion about women in the arts **:** **" women will be forgotten if they forget to think about themselves . (14)** **"**

Capitalization

Always capitalize the following:

1 • The pronoun *I* and the first word of every sentence

2 • The days of the week, the months, and holidays

| Thursday | June 15 | Labour Day |

3 • The names of specific places, such as buildings, streets, parks, public squares, lakes, rivers, cities, provinces, and countries

| Elm Street | Lake Louise | Winnipeg, Manitoba |

4 • The names of specific companies, buildings, and departments

| Morrow High School | the Finance Department | Apple Computer |

5 • The names of languages, nationalities, tribes, races, and religions

| Greek | Mohawk | Muslim |

6 • The titles of specific individuals

| General Dallaire | Prime Minister Blair | Doctor Kildaire |

7 • Course and program titles

| Economics 201 | Electrical Engineering | Beginner's Spanish |

8 • The major words in titles

| *Great Expectations* | *Lord of the Flies* | *Prison Break* |

9 • Historical events, eras, and movements

| World War II | Cubism | Baby Boomers |

Capitalization
Most capitalization rules apply to specific individuals, places, or courses. If you make a general reference without giving a specific name, capitalization is unnecessary.

a street   the school   the company   a science course

EXERCISE 7 › Add twenty missing capital letters to the following paragraphs.

1• In the last century, each generation was anointed with a title. F. Scott Fitzgerald named his cohorts when he wrote the book, *The Jazz Age*, which described 1920s flappers who frequented jazz clubs. Tom Brokaw, in his book *The Greatest Generation*, discussed people who grew up during the Great Depression. However, perhaps the most well-known spokesperson for a generation is Douglas Coupland.

2• Coupland was born in december, 1961, in Vancouver. He speaks english, german, and some italian. He graduated from Sentinal Secondary School. Then he studied sculpture at Emily Carr institute of Art and Design, which is on Johnston street in Vancouver. He also studied at the European Design institute in Italy. As a sculptor, Coupland had some success, and in november, 1987, he had a solo show called "The Floating World" at a Vancouver art gallery. Coupland had a second, more successful career as a writer. In 1991, he wrote a novel about his generation called *Generation X*.

Punctuating Titles

Place the title of a short work in quotation marks. Capitalize the major words in a title. Some examples of short works include:

essays	magazine articles	newspaper articles
poems	short stories	songs

In both "The Chaser" and "The Story of an Hour," the main character faces a dilemma.

Underline (or italicize—if you are using a computer) the title of a longer document. Some examples of longer documents include:

books	magazines	newspapers
plays	TV shows or movies	works of art

In The Departed, the main characters were in conflict. A reporter for The Montreal Gazette described the tension in the film.

EXERCISE 8 〉 Add nine missing capital letters and punctuate five titles.

1• Kurt Vonnegut was born on November 11, 1922. His novels have been published in thirty languages including Greek and Mandarin. His most popular novels are Slaughterhouse Five and Breakfast of Champions. Last year, an article about Vonnegut appeared in the magazine Atlantic Monthly. The article was called "Breakfast with a Champion." In the article, Vonnegut discussed his cameo appearance in the film Mother Night.

EXERCISE 9 〉 Correct the errors involving punctuation or capitalization in the following sentences. The number of errors in each sentence is indicated in brackets.

Example: [1] _What's_ Whats the source of creativity?

1• [2] Jamilla was worried: "I don't understand why you are leaving college?".

2• [1] Omar replied, "I need to try and make it as a musician."

3• [2] "How will you make a living in the arts", she asked?

4• [3] Omar was shocked: "I'm simply following your advice. You always say, 'Find work that you love.'"✗

5• [2] His mother suggested that Omar read the book Inner Artist.

6• [4] Omar asked, "Did you see the article about creativity called "The Left Brain" in the Vancouver Sun newspaper"?

7• [5] The following January, Omar was accepted into the Academy of Fine Arts, on Wellington street.

〉 **Take Another Look**

Answer the following questions. If you don't know an answer, go back and review the appropriate section.

Add punctuation to the following sentences.

1• Most humans believe in life after death they want to believe that life has meaning.

2• My mother always says don't believe everything that you read.

3• Last month, I read the following <u>The war of the worlds</u>, <u>1984</u>, and <u>Animal farm</u>.

4• In december, they celebrated twenty five years of marriage.

5• I read an article in the <u>Boston Globe</u> called Spirit World.

Final Review

Part A
Circle the letter of the correct answer. Note that *X* means "nothing."

1• Some cultures celebrate the end of childhood with ceremonies including … Bar or Bat Mitzvahs, graduation ceremonies, or sweet sixteen parties.

   a) ;   **b)** :   **c)** X

2• At Kara's graduation party, she received the following … clothing, jewelry, and money.

   a) ;   **b)** :   **c)** X

3• Kara is self-sufficient … "I pay my own expenses …

   a) : / "!   **b)** , / !"   **c)** : / !"

4• She read an interesting story called …

   a) "Toggling the switch."   **b)** "Toggling the Switch."   **c)** <u>Toggling the Switch.</u>

5• In her essay on youths who remain with their parents, journalist Soon Yi Phem said … "They enjoy the <u>financial</u> and emotional comfort of home …

   a) , / " (10).   **b)** : / ." (10)   **c)** : / " (10).

Part B
Underline or add quotation marks to five titles. Also correct fifteen other errors involving punctuation or capitalization.

6• Last January , an article about Dr. James Vaupels research appeared in <u>The Moncton Journal</u>. The article was called "Living Forever." Dr. Vaupel, a researcher at Duke University believes that our life span's can be extended significantly. He has frequently written for the magazine Science.

7• In 1840, Swedish women had the worlds longest life expectancy, the average Swedish woman lived to age forty five. Today, Japanese women have a life expectancy of eighty five. Sayumi Kiyoka will be ninety next friday. In an interview with the magazine Basic <u>l</u>iving, in an article called Eternity, she spoke about her lifestyle. She said: "we eat a lot of fresh fish, tofu, and miso".

Spelling and Word Choice

Spelling

Spelling Rules

Review the next spelling rules to help you become a better speller.

Writing *-gth* or *–ght*

The past forms of many verbs end in *-ght*. In such words, the *gh* is silent. Thus, *thought* is pronounced *thot*.

bou**ght**   cau**ght**

Other words end in *-gth*. When you pronounce the following words, ensure that you pronounce the final *th* by pushing your tongue slightly between your front teeth.

stren**gth**   len**gth**

Writing *ie* or *ei*

To learn the spelling of words containing *ie* or *ei*, learn the next rhyme.

Write *i* before *e*, except after *c*, or when *ei* is pronounced as *ay*, as in *neighbour* and *weigh*.

i before *e*:	bel**ie**ve	f**ie**ld
ei after *c*:	rec**ei**ve	c**ei**ling
ei pronounced as *ay*:	w**ei**gh	v**ei**n

Note that there are several exceptions to the *ie* rule.

ancient	foreign	leisure	science	society
either	height	neither	seize	weird

Adding Prefixes and Suffixes

A prefix is added to the beginning of a word, and it changes the word's meaning. When you add a prefix to a word, keep the last letter of the prefix and the first letter of the main word. Some common prefixes include *dis-*, *il-*, *im-*, *in-*, *mis-*, *non-*, and *re-*.

u**n** + **n**atural = u**nn**atural   mi**s** + **s**pell = mi**ss**pell

A **suffix** is added to the ending of a word, and it changes the word's tense or meaning. When you add the suffix *-ly* to a word that ends in *l*, keep the *l* of the root word. The new word will have two *l*s. If the word ends in *e*, keep the *e*.

fina**l** + **l**y = fina**ll**y   sur**e** + ly = sur**e**ly

Tip

Words Ending in -ful
Although the word *full* ends in two *l*s, when *full* is added to another word as a suffix, it ends in only one *l*.

beautiful   peaceful   wonderful

Exception: Notice the unusual spelling when *full* and *fill* are combined: *fulfill*.

EXERCISE 1 ❯ Underline the correctly spelled words below.

1 • <u>receive</u> / recieve	6 • disatisfied / <u>dissatisfied</u>	11 • definitly / <u>definitely</u>
2 • <u>friend</u> / freind	7 • usefull / <u>useful</u>	12 • <u>unlawful</u> / unlawfull
3 • cieling / <u>ceiling</u>	8 • <u>really</u> / realy	13 • <u>fulfill</u> / fullfil
4 • <u>thief</u> / theif	9 • strenght / <u>strength</u>	14 • ilegal / <u>illegal</u>
5 • hieght / <u>height</u>	10 • <u>fought</u> / fougth	15 • powerfull / <u>powerful</u>

Commonly Misspelled Words

The following words appear similar to words in other languages, and they are frequently misspelled. Memorize the spelling of each term. (A more complete list of commonly misspelled words appears in the *Open Road Grammar Charts*.)

address	example	ninth
aggressive	family	personality
apartment	future	potential
committed	government	questioned
developed	heroes	recommendation
embarrassed	human	responsibility
environment	interesting	responsible
exaggerated	medicine	successful

Tip

Canadian, British, and American Spelling
Not all English nations spell words the same way. Canada, which has British roots but proximity to the United States, is a hybrid nation regarding spelling. Canada retains some British rules, but has also adopted some American spelling practices.

Canada	**Great Britain**	**United States**
colour	colour	color
metre	metre	meter
realize	realise	realize

EXERCISE 2 ❯ Underline and correct fifteen spelling mistakes in the paragraphs below.

medicine
Example: Some doctors give <u>medecine</u> to hyperactive children.

aggressive
1• If a child acts in an <u>agressive</u> manner to an authority figure, parents should react.

Unfortunatly, some parents simply blame their child's misbehaviour on his or her

personality   *exagerate*   *illogical*
<u>personnality</u>. They think that others <u>exagerrate</u> about their poor or <u>ilogical</u> parenting

choices.

2• To cope with vandalism, and to discourage youths from futur damage to property,

some provinces and states have enacted parental responsability statutes. Such laws

legally   *example*
make parents <u>legaly</u> accountable for their children's criminal acts. For <u>exemple</u>, the

first parents who were ever convicted under such laws were from St. Claire Shores,

embarrassed
Michigan. They were <u>embarased</u> when, in 1995, their sixteen-year-old son

committed
<u>commited</u> a series of crimes after he was released from juvenile detention. He

apartment   *questioned*
vandalized several <u>apartement</u> buildings. The state <u>questionned</u> why the parents

successful
couldn't control their son. The prosecutor was <u>successfull</u> in convicting the parents,

and the case brought national attention to the issue.

3• Since then, some parents in Canada and the United States have been convicted and

Interestingly
fined or jailed for the crimes of their children. <u>Interestingly</u>, some of the convicted

parents were supportive of the law until their children got into trouble.

Spelling Two-Part Words

Some indefinite pronouns sound as if they should be two separate words, but they
are only one.
• Words with *any*:   *anything, anyone, anybody, anywhere*
• Words with *some*:   *something, someone, somebody, somewhere*
• Words with *every*:   *everything, everyone, everybody, everywhere*

> **Tip**
>
> **Another and A Lot**
> *Another* is always one word.   Bonnie committed <u>another</u> crime.
> *A lot* is always two words.   She robbed <u>a lot</u> of banks.

EXERCISE 3 ❯ Underline and correct nine spelling mistakes in the paragraphs below.

Another

Example: <u>An other</u> scandal occurred last year.

A lot

1• <u>Alot</u> of professional athletes have disappointed fans. <u>Some times</u> the crimes aren't

very serious. For instance, Florida State football player Peter Warrick was charged

with theft in a designer clothing scheme. Pete Rose is an other athlete who let

immoral

greed draw him into <u>imoral</u> activities when he bet against his own team.

2• However, some athletes have assaulted, raped, or even killed. Ice skater Tonya

Somebody

Harding hired <u>some body</u> to hit her skating rival in the knee. Boxer Mike Tyson was

eventually

accused and <u>eventualy</u> convicted of rape, and several professional football players

have been charged with murder.

3• Because television and newspapers present professional athletes as icons, many

anything

fans refuse to accept that their heros have done <u>any thing</u> wrong. Basketball fan

Anybody

Trevor Nixon says, "<u>Any body</u> can make accusations." Perhaps the public should

accept that athletes are not always heroic.

> **Tip**
>
> **Use Spell-Check**
> When you type on the computer, take advantage of the spell-check feature. If you are
> using Word, the *Spelling and Grammar* tool will underline most misspelled words using a
> wavy red line. Right-click on the mouse and review the spelling options and choose the
> appropriate spelling.
>
> Be aware that a spell-check's abilities are limited; it cannot verify if you have used
> commonly confused words accurately. For example, it can't differentiate between the
> words *their* and *there*.

Word Choice

Standard English

In both academic and professional writing, you should use **standard English**.
Standard English is the common language generally used and expected in schools,
businesses, and government institutions.

Avoid Slang

Slang is non-standard language that is used in informal situations. In academic writing, it is preferable to use more formal terms. Review the following slang words.

cool	guy	dude	kid	psyched	stuff

Slang: The <u>kid</u> had a lot of <u>stuff</u> under his bed.

Better: The <u>child</u> had a lot of <u>toys, clothing, and books</u> under his bed.

Avoid Vague Language

People often use vague or imprecise words. For example, if you call a story "good," the reader doesn't get a clear picture of what you mean. The following words are vague.

bad	good	great	nice	thing

Vague: "The Chaser" is a <u>good</u> story.

Precise: "The Chaser" is an <u>entertaining tale about a man who wants to control his girlfriend's emotions</u>.

EXERCISE 4 Underline and edit ten examples of slang and vague language in the following paragraphs. Replace the slang or vague language with more formal and precise terms.

man

Example: The old <u>dude</u> was really surprised.

1. In the Stanford Prison Experiment, some regular <u>guys</u> *men* agreed to play the role of prisoners, and others played the role of the prison guards. The "prisoners" weren't allowed to bring any of their own <u>stuff</u> *materials* into the simulated prison.

2. Originally, Philippe Zimbardo, the experimenter, thought the guards would show some <u>TLC</u> to the prisoners, but he was really shocked when some of the guards started acting like total <u>jerks</u>. They did some bad <u>stuff</u> to the prisoners.

3. One of the guards, for instance, was totally <u>not cool</u> *mean*. He became <u>like the big man</u> *the leader*, and he started making rules that were <u>dumb</u> *stupid*. The crazy part is almost all the other guards started to copy him. The men who were the prisoners became, like, really <u>whipped</u>.

Commonly Confused Words

Review the following list of words that sound alike but have very different meanings.

accept	to receive or to admit	You should really <u>accept</u> my apology.
except	excluding or other than	Everyone <u>except</u> Lauren was at the movie.
allowed	permitted	The children aren't <u>allowed</u> to stay up past nine.
aloud	spoken audibly	We couldn't speak <u>aloud</u>, so we whispered.
considered	contemplated; thought out	He was <u>considered</u> the main suspect in the case.
considerate	kind and understanding	His lawyer was a very gentle and <u>considerate</u> person.
hole	an opening through something	There is a large <u>hole</u> where the house used to be.
whole	the full amount	The company tore down the <u>whole</u> house.
lose	to misplace something (past form: *lost*)	I often <u>lose</u> my keys.
loose	not tight; baggy	My pants are too <u>loose</u>. I need a belt.
loss	a decrease in value	The company suffered a <u>loss</u> for the third year in a row.
price	the cost of something	The sofa is on sale for a very good <u>price</u>.
prize	a reward for winning a contest	He won the contest, and his <u>prize</u> was a trip to Hawaii.
sell	to transfer something in exchange for money	The new hardware store <u>sells</u> tires.
sale	a reduced price	The tires were on <u>sale</u> for fifty percent off.

EXERCISE 5 ⟩ Underline the correct words in parentheses below.

Example: What have you got to (loose / <u>lose</u>)? Take a chance!

1 • Most people, (accept / <u>except</u>) for a privileged few, will be fired or laid off at some point in their lives. When you (loose / <u>lose</u>) a job, it is important to remain focused. You must (<u>accept</u> / except) what happened and not dwell on it. You have your (<u>whole</u> / hole) life in front of you.

2 • My sisters (<u>sell</u> / sale) cosmetics. They are very good saleswomen, and they are never at a (lost / <u>loss</u>) for words. Because they represent a large manufacturer, they are (aloud / <u>allowed</u>) to buy many items on (sell / <u>sale</u>). For example, the (prize / <u>price</u>) for very good skin cream is only $10 a bottle. However, last week they both (loss / <u>lost</u>) a major client because the company they were selling to suffered a rather large financial (lose / <u>lost</u> / loss) and needed to cut corners.

3 • Still, my sisters love to (sale / <u>sell</u>) cosmetics. Their boss, Mrs. Wiley, is very (considered / <u>considerate</u>), and she treats her employees very well. Last summer, my younger sister won a (<u>prize</u> / price) because she sold the most cosmetics in her division. She won a day at a spa.

4 • Yesterday, the company's maintenance worker spent the (<u>whole</u> / hole) day repairing a problem outdoors. There was a large (whole / <u>hole</u>) in the parking lot. A manager accidentally drove into the (whole / <u>hole</u>) and damaged her front axle. She (<u>considered</u> / considerate) suing the company for damages to her car.

More Commonly Confused Words

Some words may look like words in your language. However, the meaning in English may not match the meaning in your language. Memorize the following words and their meanings.

Rob and *Steal*

Both *rob* and *steal* mean "to take property illegally." However, *to steal* is to take an entire object. *To rob* is to take something from the object. Notice the difference in meaning.

He **robbed** the car.   He took the valuables, such as the CD player, from the car.

He **stole** the car.   He took the car.

Learn and *Teach*

The person discovering information *learns*. The person providing the information *teaches*.

He **learned** how to read when he was five. His mother **taught** him how to read.

Leave and *Quit*

You *quit* a job or position. You can't *quit* a person. However, you can *leave* a person or place.

He plans to **leave** his wife after ten years of marriage. Then he will **quit** his job and move to an island.

Memory, *Remind*, *Remember*, and *Souvenir*

Memory is a noun meaning "the capacity to retain past impressions." It can also refer to the past impressions themselves. *Remind* is a verb meaning "to cause a person to remember something." *Remember* is a verb meaning "to recall." A *souvenir* is a memento that you buy to remind yourself of a special place.

When we went to New York, we brought back a **souvenir** of the Statue of Liberty. I **remember** many details about our trip. Please **remind** me to call my grandmother and tell her about it. She is eighty, but she has a great **memory**. She has fond **memories** of the first time she saw the Statue of Liberty.

Say and *Tell*

Use *say* in direct and indirect quotations. Follow *say* with the actual words that were said. *Tell* is followed by a noun or pronoun. You must tell <u>somebody</u> something.

Alex **said**, "Let's move to Nova Scotia." He **told** <u>me</u> that he wanted to move to Halifax.

EXERCISE 6 ❯ Underline and correct one error involving commonly confused words in each of the sentences below. Write *C* beside the sentences that are correct.

1 • If you try to control your girlfriend, you will <u>loose</u> her. *lose* ▪ She might <u>quit</u> you. *leave* ▪ Mr. Tyler <u>learned</u> me that I sometimes have to let go of loved ones. *taught* ▪ He <u>said</u> me a lot of interesting things. *tell* ▪ For instance, he said that if I spend my <u>hole</u> life regretting past errors, then life could pass me by. *whole* ▪ To help me get over a heartbreak, I decided to go to Europe with my cousin. *C* ▪

2 • When my cousin and I went to Amsterdam, we were <u>stolen</u>. *robbed* ▪ We were too inattentive, and a man took all of our credit cards. *C* ▪ Did you know that you are <u>aloud</u> to have a personal identification number on your credit card? *allowed* ▪ Please <u>remember</u> me to get a PIN number when my new credit card arrives. *remind* ▪ I don't have a very good <u>souvenir,</u> and I often forget important information. *memory* ▪

3 • I'm not very upset about the robbery. *C* ▪ My souvenirs about the theft are actually good ones. *C* ▪ The event was funny because my cousin was trying to <u>learn</u> me how to drive a scooter. *teach* ▪ At that moment, the robber was <u>quitting</u> a store, and he headed straight for us. *leaving* ▪ He spoke <u>allowed</u> and asked us for our wallets. *aloud* ▪ My brother and I were at a lost for words. *C* ▪ We just handed him our wallets. *C* ▪ Afterwards, we looked at each other and both <u>told</u>, "Why did we just give him our money?" *said* ▪

Prepositional Expressions

Many verbs are followed by certain prepositions. Memorize the following prepositional expressions. A more complete list of verb/preposition combinations appears in your *Open Road Grammar Charts*.

apologize for	consist of	look at	responsible for
ask for	depend on	participate in	scared of
believe in	insist on	prepared for	search for
capable of	interested in	rely on	specialize in

Toni was <u>responsible</u> *for* the accident.

They <u>depend</u> *on* science to answer difficult questions.

EXERCISE 7 ❭ Fill in the blanks with appropriate prepositions.

Example: My father really depends __*on*__ my mother.

1 • In times of need, can we depend ___*on*___ others to help us? A part of the brain, called the limbic system, is responsible ___*for*___ our emotional reactions. In the past, some scientists believed that humans were not capable ___*of*___ altruistic behaviour until they were properly socialized and their brains were fairly developed. However, some intriguing studies suggest that helpful behaviour begins at a very early age.

2 • Felix Warneken and Mike Tomasello are researchers who specialize ___*in*___ human behaviour, and they are interested ___*in*___ altruism. They developed scenarios in which an adult wasn't capable ___*of*___ solving a simple problem. Some very young children participated ___*in*___ the experiments. In one study, Warneken hung clothing on a line and then dropped a peg that was out of his reach while a baby played nearby. He looked ___*at*___ the baby, but he didn't ask ___*for*___ help. Over 80 percent of the time, the baby would pick up the peg and hand it to him.

3 • In another version of the experiment, Warneken threw the peg on the ground. In those tests, the babies appeared to be scared ___*of*___ him, and they didn't pick up the item. The babies only helped Warneken when they knew that he needed help to complete his goal of hanging the clothes.

4 • The experiments indicate that infants with very little socialization or language skills are willing to help others. They feel responsible ___*for*___ the well-being of people around them. Such studies help explain why human beings can rely ___*on*___ each other in times of need.

❭ Take Another Look

Answer the following questions. If you don't know an answer, go back and review the appropriate section.

1 • Underline the correctly spelled words in the pairs below.

   a) nineth / ninth   **c)** naturally / naturaly   **e)** responsible / responsable

   b) fulfil / fulfill   **d)** adress / address   **f)** government / governement

2 • Underline and correct the errors in the sentences below.

   a) You might win a price if you buy a ticket for the contest. _____

   b) My coach said me to work harder. _____

   c) I need to sale some of my old hockey equipment. _____

   d) Tony is responsible of the boy's death. _____

Final Review

→

Part A

Correct the misspelled words below. Write *C* next to the words that are spelled correctly.

Example: shure _____*sure*_____

1 • unusualy _____*unusually*_____   7 • recommandation _____*C*_____

2 • writting _____*C*_____   8 • another _____*C*_____

3 • exaggerated _____*C*_____   9 • alot _____*a lot*_____

4 • personnality _____*personality*_____   10 • questionning _____*questioning*_____

5 • responsability _____*C*_____   11 • definitly _____*definitely*_____

6 • strenght _____*strength*_____   12 • finally _____*C*_____

Part B

Underline and correct eight errors involving word choice in the paragraphs below.

13 • Some ordinary people do extraordinary acts. Recently, somebody remembered [*reminded*] me of a very important moment. In 1989, students in China wanted to live in a more democratic nation. They thought they would have nothing to loose [*lose*] if they made a peaceful protest in Tiananmen Square, which is in central Beijing.

》》》 China's unknown rebel

14 • On June 4, army tanks entered the square, and soldiers opened fire on the protesters. Remarkably, one unknown man did a very brave act. He stood calmly in front of a line of tanks and refused to quit [*leave*] the road. The tanks stopped, and journalists took pictures of the brave man. That unknown rebel is considerate [*considered*] a true hero. He may have paid the ultimate prize [*price*] for his act of disobedience.

15 • Some observers told [*said*] that the rebellious man was imprisoned and tortured for his action. Today, those people who lived through the massacre have very bad souvenirs of June 4, 1989. In schools, teachers should learn [*teach*] students about the massacre in Tiananmen Square.

Review
of Units 7 to 12

Class Exercise A
Pronouns, Plurals, and Determiners

Each sentence below contains zero, one, or two errors. Underline and correct the errors involving plurals, pronouns, and determiners such as *much* and *many* in the sentences below. Write *C* beside the sentences that are correct.

1 • Last year, a fifty-million-dollars production was filmed in our city.   _____

2 • One of Hollywood's most well-known actor was here.   _____

3 • A few persons in our local economy benefited tremendously.   _____

4 • For example, Simon Ross, who owns a two-levels building on

   Esplanade Avenue, rents his home to much different film studios.   _____

5 • Although many people in the film world entered his home,

   Ross was well compensated for the inconvenience.   _____

6 • He was given two thousand dollars per day for the use of his home.   _____

7 • He says that this days of filming made his life very exciting last year.   _____

8 • He fondly remembers every moments of that time.   _____

9 • My brother and me are interested in filmmaking, and we have

   written many scripts by ourself.   _____

10 • I admit that my brother did a little more work than me.   _____

11 • In the 1990s, we were quite successful, and we sold three

   different kind of scripts to studios.   _____

12 • We sold our first script when my brother was a twenty-years-old student.   _____

13• In the past, we earned about five thousand dollars for each script. _____

14• Since 2000, we have sold less stories than we sold in previous years. _____

15• Too much film companies make big-screen adaptations

of bad televisions programs from the 1970s. _____

Class Exercise B
Passive Voice, Gerunds, Infinitives, and Comparative Forms

Underline the appropriate word in parentheses.

Example: The book *Business Ethics* was (publishing / publish / <u>published</u>) by Prentice Hall in 2006.

1• The book *Business Ethics*, (write / wrote / <u>written</u>) by G. T. George, describes a famous product defect case. In the early 1970s, Japanese automakers succeeded (entering / to enter / in entering) the North American marketplace, and many people stopped (to drive / driving) American cars because they preferred the (most / more / more better) fuel-efficient Japanese imports. To compete with the imports flooding the market, Lee Iacocca, the CEO of Ford Motor Company, was enthusiastic (to produce / producing / about producing) an economic and lightweight car. In 1970, engineers developed the Ford Pinto.

2• Because Ford wanted the product on the market (real quick / really quickly / really quick), the car wasn't (testing / <u>tested</u>) for rear-end impact during the production period. After the Pintos had been produced, they were (drive / drove / <u>driven</u>) in collision tests, and they failed the tests. When the Pinto (hitted / hit / <u>was hit</u>) from behind, a bolt on the bumper sometimes punctured the fuel tank, which could cause an explosion.

3• Ford conducted a study and determined that a small baffle, worth about eight dollars, could be (placing / placed / place) between the bumper and the gas tank. The company decided (to conduct / conducting) a cost-benefit analysis to compare the cost of adding the baffle against the estimated cost of lawsuits. The company decided that it was (more better / better / best) to fight lawsuits than to insert the baffle. For the next seven years, the company did not consider (to change / changing / on changing) the design of Ford Pintos. The company decided (to don't offer / <u>not to offer</u>) the baffle to customers.

4• In 1976, Pintos had thirteen explosions from rear-end impacts, which was twice the number of explosions for cars of a comparable size. The Ford Motor Company spent millions of dollars on lawsuits and realized it was much (worst / worser / worse) to fight the lawsuits than to install the baffle installations. The Pinto was recalled in 1978.

Class Exercise C
Sentences and Punctuation

Underline and correct the errors involving sentence form or punctuation. Note that the number of errors in each sentence is indicated in brackets.

1 • [2] Grigory Rasputin was born on january 10, 1869, in a small siberian town.

2 • [1] He loved alcohol and sex, he consumed both in excess.

3 • [1] Rasputin was close to Russia's royal family.

4 • [1] He often wondered why do they trusted him.

5 • [1] He knew how to hypnotize people and how to ~~reading~~ read minds.

6 • [1] He was able to help the Tsar's only son, nobody knows how he did it.

7 • [2] An article about Rasputin appeared in an issue of Atlantic monthly.

8 • [4] The title of the article is Russia's holy mystic.

9 • [2] The author claims that Rasputin and Tsarina Aleksandra weren't lovers, "Although many people gossiped about their affair, the rumours were without foundation".

10 • [1] Several books who discuss Rasputin have been published.

Class Exercise D
Tense Review

Write the verbs in parentheses in the correct tense. Then make the verb negative and write a question that asks for information. (The exact answer is in bold). Finally, explain why the tense was used. Note that you shouldn't use the same verb tense twice.

Example: Violet (eat) ____eats____ **meat**. Negative: ____does not eat____
Question: __What does Violet eat?__
Reason: ____The action is a fact.____

1 • Maya (love) _____ **to travel**.

Negative: _____

Question: _____

Reason: _____

2• She (go) _____ to Chile **last summer**.

Negative: _____

Question: _____

Reason: _____

3• Maya (live) _____ in Chile **since then.**

Negative: _____

Question: _____

Reason: _____

4• Last July, while she (walk) _____ **on a beach**, she saw a shark.

Negative: _____

Question: _____

Reason: _____

5• Yes, she (see, already) _____ a shark before then.

Negative: _____

Question: _____

Reason: _____

6• Next July, we (visit) _will visit_ Maya.

Negative: _won't visit_

Question: _when will you visit Maya?_

Reason: _We miss her_

7• Right now she (write) _____ about **her trip**.

Negative: _____

Question: _____

Reason: _____

Appendix
Irregular Verb List

BASE FORM	SIMPLE PAST	PAST PARTICIPLE	BASE FORM	SIMPLE PAST	PAST PARTICIPLE
arise	arose	arisen	fall	fell	fallen
be	was / were	been	feed	fed	fed
bear	bore	borne / born	feel	felt	felt
beat	beat	beat / beaten	fight	fought	fought
become	became	become	find	found	found
begin	began	begun	flee	fled	fled
bend	bent	bent	fling	flung	flung
bet	bet	bet	fly	flew	flown
bind	bound	bound	forbid	forbade	forbidden
bite	bit	bitten	forget	forgot	forgotten
bleed	bled	bled	forgive	forgave	forgiven
blow	blew	blown	forsake	forsook	forsaken
break	broke	broken	freeze	froze	frozen
breed	bred	bred	get	got	got / gotten
bring	brought	brought	give	gave	given
build	built	built	go	went	gone
burst	burst	burst	grind	ground	ground
buy	bought	bought	grow	grew	grown
cast	cast	cast	hang	hung	hung
catch	caught	caught	have	had	had
choose	chose	chosen	hear	heard	heard
cling	clung	clung	hide	hid	hidden
come	came	come	hit	hit	hit
cost	cost	cost	hold	held	held
creep	crept	crept	hurt	hurt	hurt
cut	cut	cut	keep	kept	kept
deal	dealt	dealt	kneel	knelt	knelt
dig	dug	dug	know	knew	known
do	did	done	lay	laid	laid
draw	drew	drawn	lead	led	led
drink	drank	drunk	leave	left	left
drive	drove	driven	lend	lent	lent
eat	ate	eaten	let	let	let

BASE FORM	SIMPLE PAST	PAST PARTICIPLE	BASE FORM	SIMPLE PAST	PAST PARTICIPLE
lie[1]	lay	lain	speak	spoke	spoken
light	lit	lit	speed	sped	sped
lose	lost	lost	spend	spent	spent
make	made	made	spin	spun	spun
mean	meant	meant	spit	spit / spat	spit
meet	met	met	split	split	split
mistake	mistook	mistaken	spread	spread	spread
pay	paid	paid	spring	sprang	sprung
prove	proved	proved / proven	stand	stood	stood
put	put	put	steal	stole	stolen
quit	quit	quit	stick	stuck	stuck
read	read	read	sting	stung	stung
rid	rid	rid	stink	stank	stunk
ride	rode	ridden	strike	struck	struck
ring	rang	rung	swear	swore	sworn
rise	rose	risen	sweep	swept	swept
run	ran	run	swell	swelled	swollen
say	said	said	swim	swam	swum
see	saw	seen	swing	swung	swung
sell	sold	sold	take	took	taken
send	sent	sent	teach	taught	taught
set	set	set	tear	tore	torn
shake	shook	shaken	tell	told	told
shed	shed	shed	think	thought	thought
shine	shone	shone	throw	threw	thrown
shoot	shot	shot	thrust	thrust	thrust
show	showed	shown	understand	understood	understood
shut	shut	shut	upset	upset	upset
shrink	shrank	shrunk	wake	woke	woken
sing	sang	sung	wear	wore	worn
sink	sank	sunk	weep	wept	wept
sit	sat	sat	win	won	won
sleep	slept	slept	wind	wound	wound
slide	slid	slid	withdraw	withdrew	withdrawn
slit	slit	slit	write	wrote	written

1 *Lie* can mean "to rest in a flat position." When *lie* means "tell a false statement," it is a regular verb: *lie, lied, lied.*

Note: some verbs have both regular and irregular past tense forms.

burn: burned / burnt	dream: dreamed / dreamt	learn: learn / learnt
dive: dived / dove	dwell: dwelled / dwelt	spoil: spoiled / spoilt

Appendix
Citing Sources Using
the MLA Style

Each time you use another writer's words or ideas, you must **cite the source**, which means that you give complete information about the source from which you borrowed the material. You should mention the source in the body of your work and on a "Works Cited" page.

In-Text Citations

When you cite the source in the body of your essay, you can use **parenthetical citations** (you offset the source information using parentheses). Introduce the author's name or the story's title in the text and write the page reference in parentheses. Place the final period after the parentheses.

> In "My African Childhood," David Sedaris writes, "Certain events are parallel, but compared with Hugh's, my childhood was unspeakably dull" (63).

> According to sociologist David S. Locher, "Violent mobs often take out their anger and frustration on any individual" (92).

> **Tip**
>
> **Citing Certain Web Sources**
> If you are using a web-based source, no page number is necessary. If you don't know the author's name, put the title of the site in parentheses.
>
> Jazz is not purely American: "Jazz is a musical art form rooted in West African cultural and musical expression and in the African American blues tradition" ("Jazz History").

Making a Works Cited Page

To prepare a Works Cited page using the MLA format, follow the directions below.

1 • Write *Works Cited* at the top of the page and centre it.

2 • List each source alphabetically, using the last names of the authors.

3 • Indent the second line and all subsequent lines of each reference.

These are some examples of how to cite different types of publications:

Book

Carefully review the punctuation of the following example.

> Last name, First name. <u>Title of the Book</u>. Edition. Place of Publication: Publisher, Year.

Findley, Timothy. <u>Famous Last Words</u>. Toronto: Penguin, 1982.

If there is more than one author, reverse the name of the first author but not the subsequent authors.

Ember, Carol R. and Melvin Ember. <u>Cultural Anthropology</u>. New Jersey: Prentice Hall, 2002.

When your source is a story or article inside a book, start with the name of the article's author and the title of the article, followed by the title of the book and the author of the book. If the book is a second, third, or subsequent edition, write just the abbreviated form of the edition (2nd ed.) after the title.

Gifford, Alicia. "Toggling the Switch." <u>Open Road English Skills</u>. 2nd Ed. By Lynne Gaetz. St. Laurent: Pearson Longman, 2007.

When encyclopedias and dictionaries list items alphabetically, you can omit volume and page numbers. It is sufficient to list the edition and year of publication.

"Democracy." <u>Columbia Encyclopedia</u>. 6th ed. 2005.

Magazine or Newspaper

> Last name, First name. "Title of Article." <u>Title of the Magazine or Newspaper</u> Date: Pages.

Geddes, Don. "Canadian Combat." <u>Macleans</u> 20 March 2006: 21–22.

Internet Source

Include as much of the following information as you can find. Keep in mind that some sites don't provide complete information.

> Last name, First name. "Title of Article." <u>Title of Site or Online Publication</u>. Date of publication. Date you went on the site <Network Address>.

Krystek, Lee. "Crop Circles." <u>Museum of Unnatural Mystery</u>. 2003. 16 May 2007 <http://www.unmuseum.org/cropcir.htm>.

If the author isn't mentioned on the site, just begin with the title and include as much information as you can find.

"The Canadian Refugee System." <u>Citizenship and Immigration Canada</u>. 2005. 28 May 2006 <http://www.cic.gc.ca/english/refugees/index.html>.

Tip

Placement and Order of Works Cited
The Works Cited page should appear at the end of your essay. List sources in alphabetical order of the author's last names. If there is no author, list the title (but ignore the *a*, *an*, or *the* which may appear at the beginning of the title).

Calvino, Italo. "Conscience." <u>Open Road English Skills</u>. 2nd ed. By Lynne Gaetz. St. Laurent: Pearson Longman, 2007.

Gifford, Alicia. "Toggling the Switch." <u>Open Road English Skills</u>. 2nd ed. By Lynne Gaetz. St. Laurent: Pearson Longman, 2007.

"Smashed: Drugs and Driving." <u>Statistics Canada</u>. 2005. 14 April 2008 <http://www.tc.gc.ca/roadsafety/tp/tp1535/drugs.htm>.

Appendix
Spelling and
Grammar Logs

Spelling and Grammar Logs can help you stop repeating the same errors. When you do new writing assignments, you can consult the lists and hopefully break some bad habits.

Spelling Log

Every time you misspell a word, record both the mistake and the correction in your spelling log. Then, before you hand in a writing assignment, consult the list of misspelled words. The goal is to stop repeating the same spelling errors.

Example: **Incorrect**   **Correct**

responsable   responsible

futur   future

Grammar Log

Each time a writing assignment is returned to you, identify one or two repeated errors and add them to your grammar log. Then, consult the grammar log before you hand in writing assignments in order to avoid making the same errors. For each type of grammar error, you could do the following:

1) Identify the assignment and write down the type of error.
2) In your own words, write a rule about the error.
3) Include an example from your writing assignment.

Example: <u>Writing Test 1</u> (Oct. 2)   Run-On

Don't join two complete sentences with a comma.

complex. Nations
The causes of war are complex, nations sometimes declare war for economic reasons.

Index